Understanding
Everyday Life in Korea

Understanding Everyday Life in Korea

Brief Answers to 80 FAQs on Korea

Kim, Young Hoon

JIMOONDANG

Jimoondang

85 Gwanginsa-gil, Paju-si, Gyeonggi-do, 413-756, Korea

82 Donhwamun-ro, Jongno-gu, Seoul, 110-360, Korea

227 Suttons Lane, Edison, NJ 08817, USA

Phone: 82-2-743-3096   E-mail: edit@jimoon.co.kr

        82-2-743-3192~3   E-mail: sale@jimoon.co.kr

Fax: 82-2-743-0227, 82-2-742-4657

Homepage: www.jimoon.co.kr

The National Library of Korea Cataloging-in-Publication (CIP)

Understanding Everyday Life in Korea, 2015

By Kim, Young Hoon

Paju, Seoul and Edison: Jimoondang

ISBN 978-89-6297-171-2 (03380)

CIP2015006897

Printed in Korea

Preface

I often receive questions from international students who come to Korea as exchange students. Some of those questions embarrass me, but a lot of times I find most of their questions very interesting. Although methodology or theory is important in the study of Korean culture, I felt we also need more easy-to-read books for beginning students to pursue their curiosity on Korea. I collected 80 questions regarding Korean culture from my international students and also from the Internet. Rather than considering a particular number of questions, I have chosen questions that are related to various different aspects of Korea and I tried not to concentrate on any particular aspects. Those questions include the characteristics of Korean customs, rituals and traditional ceremonies, manners, interpersonal relations and behavior, language and values, religion and folklore, food culture, housing culture, entertainment, pop culture and other aspects about Korean life.

I had a joyful and instructive time while answering these questions. Many international students looked at things usually taken for granted by Koreans with different perspectives and often with amazement, and they wanted to have answers. Some unexpected questions, which I had not thought about, puzzled me, but most of them were insightful and interesting. Why do people in Korea like to stir and mix rice with other ingredients? It is not simple to answer this kind of question. We always search for better answers but soon we realize that one needs to start with a good question to come up with a good answer. We re-encounter Korea by receiving strange and unexpected questions. Questions asked by foreigners provide us with a chance to recognize things that had been ignored or unnoticed otherwise and cause us to see things through a different perspective. Thus, this book is not beneficial just for foreigners but also for Koreans.

To me, Korea itself is the most important and fascinating question. I am not exaggerating simply because I work as a professor and researcher in this field. Evidently, South Korea is a country that has shown incredible facts and statistics. According to the first statistics about Korea compiled by the United Nations after the Korean War in 1950, South Korea's personal income and GDP increased hundreds of times in only 50 years. It has grown to become the 11th largest economy and one of the world's largest economic markets. There has never been such a dramatic economic growth in the past and there will not be one in the near future. Korea has undergone peaceful democratic change, which is rarely found among underdeveloped countries. Not many people are aware of the fact that Korea is also the most successful country in forestation. However, Korea is the only divided country in the world and also has the largest number of people in their 40's who consider immigration to other countries. To many social scientists in the fields of economy, history, or cultural studies, Korea is an attractive topic of study full of mysteries. Where did Korea come from and where is it heading?

This book is the result of the sincerity and dedication of a number of people. I would first like to thank Yoojin Shin, Jaerin Ahn and Olga Anufrieva, both graduate students at Ewha Womans University for their assistance in translating the manuscript. Special thanks must go to Yoojin Shin again who managed the publication process on my behalf. I hope these brief answers would be a useful guide to beginners in Korean studies. I have learned a lot from their curiosity. Last, but not least, I give special thanks to my colleague, Professor Kyong-Mi Danyel Kwon for her dedication in proofreading the manuscripts and providing advice.

Contents

I

GREETING MANNERS

1 | How do Koreans greet strangers for the first time?

Different greetings in different cultures are a very fascinating practice from an anthropological point of view. Greetings are a very simple procedure which exists everywhere in a different form based on different social norms and cultures.

It is common in Korea to greet someone for the first time by saying: "*annyeong-hasimnikka cheoeum-boepgetseumnida*" meaning "Hello, I'm very pleased to meet you" in a very formal and polite way. It is followed by a self-introduction that includes the speaker's name, profession, hometown, and age which is one of the most important things to mention when meeting someone for the first time since it forms the basis of social hierarchy in Korea. The difference of age and social status between two people decides the speech style and behavior. For Westerners, it might seem weird and rude to ask such personal questions on the first meeting. Koreans, however, observe different cultural norms and thus it is very common and necessary procedure in Korea.

A simple and most common greeting, *annyeong-hasimnikka*, can be used throughout the day from morning till night. Non-verbal gestures used together with *annyeong-hasimnikka* are not as simple. Shaking hands, which is widely used in Western countries, have now become a common way of greeting in Korea. However, there are special tips to shakings hand in Korea: first, you cannot offer to shake hands with someone who is older or has a higher social position; second, when you shake hands with an older person, you should do it with two hands. If two persons are of the same age, they should greet each other in some other way rather than shaking hands. Bowing is even a more common way to greet people but different bows are used depending on one's age and social status. You can bend the whole body or just do a little bow with your head. When someone is receiving a medal or certificate from a superior, for example, he should first greet the president with a deep bow and accept his/her handshake using two hands. Of course, the superior would offer to shake hands first using just one hand. Back in the days when social hierarchy was more rigid than today, straightening up immediately after the bow was considered to be ill-mannered.

The greeting culture in Korea still reflects a strong Confucian tradition although between people of the same age it is very informal and casual. Sometimes people of the same age greet each other by lightly hitting the other's shoulders, a sign of intimacy. Sometimes, however, such greeting may seem as if they are fighting with each other. Rest assured that strangers who are meeting each other for the first time would never greet each other like this. Once they find out they are of the same age, then they may do so—to many foreigners' dismay—even when they are not on friendly terms yet.

2 | Why is it rude to call older people by their names?

In Korea, people usually don't call someone older by his or her name. The reason is very simple. There is a strict social hierarchy based on one's age. If you address someone by his or her name, it shows equality between two persons that can exist only when they are of the same age. There is a saying in Korea, *jangyuyuseo*, which means "elders first". For Confucius, one of the most effective methods of rescuing society from chaos and disorder was the principle of ethics. The major teachings of Confucianism are not difficult to understand. People should be devoted to a king, and children should have filial piety for their parents. *Hyo* and *chung*, which mean filial piety and respect for elders, may be the most familiar Chinese characters to Koreans. *Jangyuyuseo* mentioned above is also an element of Confucius' teachings and one of the Five Relationships but it does not mean that one can rule over his or her juniors. For that, one would have to earn the respect by good deeds and hence the saying: you have to pay the price of your age. Nevertheless, the younger person is always at a lower position whether or not the older person pays the price of his or her age. The older brother is the first, any older person is the first. Calling each other by their first name is considered to be a sign of intimacy and equality in Korea so it is impossible to call the older person by his or her name whether or not they are in a formal or informal situation. Usually, it is common to use the surname before the title *ssi*, which is equivalent to san in Japanese, or the profession of the person to be polite and show etiquette. Using just a title of the profession after surname is not enough so the suffix *nim* is added to show a respectful attitude. In the case of Kang who is a professor, for example, Koreans would not just call him Kang *kyeosu* but Kang *kyeosu-nim*. If the profession of the person is unknown, it is possible to use the *nim* suffix together with his or her name. The best and most safe way may be to call someone's surname with the title *seonsaengnim* which literally means 'teacher' but also a general way of addressing strangers.

However, *nim* or *seonsaengnim* cannot always solve the problem. The Korean titles system is much more complicated than can be quickly grasped at first glance. For example, what do you call a person who is older but has a lower rank in your company? What about a senior in the university who is younger than you? There are many confusing instances in which one's age and the social status don't match. That is why Korean students first introduce not the year (*haknyeon*) of the university, but *hakbeon*, which indicates one's age referring to the year when the person started his undergraduate studies. If the person is older but has a lower social status, it is common to show him respect befitting his age.

Because these rules originated in Confucianism, it is impossible to disobey teachers or start eating before the oldest person does. And it is hard to imagine calling an older person by his or her name. When I first went to study in the USA, my academic adviser told me to call him by his first name Emilio. It took me more than several months to actually start calling him that. Every time I called his name, I realized how different the cultures were from each other. For most Koreans, they would find it very difficult to call their professors or bosses by their first names even in their thoughts.

There is still a rare chance for Koreans to call older people by their names as much as they want. It is called *yaja* time game and is used to loosen very strict hierarchal social relationships. During the fixed period of time younger people can call their seniors by their first names, and when *yaja* time is over, everything is forgotten as if it never happened and thus no one can hold grudges against each other for being disrespectful. This *yaja* is the only time for people to forget the hierarchy pressure resulting from a very strict relationship determined by one's age in the Korean society. Coming from the Confucian practices of Joseon dynasty, this tradition is still very prevalent nowadays. Even the word 'friend' is only used between people of the same age. Being friends with someone who is a teacher and is ten years older may be unthinkable for Koreans.

3 | Why do Koreans ask personal questions to people they hardly know or meet for the first time?

The most popular question among foreign exchange students when they first arrive in Korea: "Why do Koreans ask so many personal questions to those whom they meet for the first time?" Soon after introducing their names, Korean people often ask the other person's age. To Koreans, it is necessary to know who is older and who is younger in order to establish a relationship with a person. Depending on one's age and social status, a style of speech and attitude is determined. If they are of the same age, they will be extremely happy because they won't have to deal with the awkwardness of a first meeting. Such reaction, in turn, may confuse and surprise a foreign student. The questions, however, don't actually stop here. Koreans often ask many more questions, including questions about marital status. If you are not married, they would ask why not and whether you are dating anyone.

Foreigners might feel uncomfortable being asked such series of seemingly personal questions and think that Koreans are rude. Some may even get hurt by these straightforward questions. They might have been divorced or separated with a lover but Koreans don't seem to care that their questions might hurt someone. Are they really so rude? Koreans would be very surprised and feel sad about such misunderstanding. Those questions which are considered to be inappropriate in Western countries would not bother Koreans at all. Koreans just ask them in order to build rapport and to show that they are interested in the other person.

In a collective Korean society, the borders between individuals are very vague. Koreans never say 'my' school, 'my' country, 'my' company, or 'my' husband. Instead, they say 'our,' or '*uri*.' The general attitude of Koreans toward each other was to exchange feelings and become one without distinguishing mine from yours so everything automatically became 'ours.' It is not just to be friendly but to build a very open and honest relationship with each other. For example, when Koreans invite guests to their house, they show every room and every corner, even their bedrooms and private bathrooms. This cultural custom shows that Koreans don't want to conceal anything from the others, and this type of attitude seems right for them. Foreign students, who stay in Korea longer, usually get used to getting many personal questions and come to understand this.

When visiting Korean friends' home, their parents usually ask very similar questions again. How many brothers or sisters do you have or what do your parents do for living and so on. Sometimes parents add some recommendations and advices about life. This can become a real culture shock. Why would a stranger whom you have just met show so much interest in your personal life and even give advice on how to live? Or, a foreigner might find his or her invited Korean guests looking around and behave as if they are at their own home. They may open a wardrobe or try on some cosmetics without asking permission first.

4 | When people meet their acquaintance by chance, why do they usually ask "where are you going?"

To put it simply, these are phatic greetings used often by Koreans. They are not actually asking where you are going or whether you've eaten yet. Similar phatic expressions are everywhere and from what I have heard, Chinese people have similar expressions of greeting. However, Koreans asking whether the person has already eaten has a special origin.

Not too long ago, people greeted elders by asking them, "Have you eaten?" instead of saying "Hello." Eating was the most pressing issue for Koreans in the agrarian days when farming was difficult and time-consuming while frequent wars exhausted both natural resources and manpower. It was thus natural for people to inquire after each other's well-being by way of asking them whether or not they have eaten already. While this explanation is quite plausible, there may be another reason?

There are not many countries like Korea where people value the experiences of eating together with others. Eating alone is unusual and much avoided while eating with a lot of people, or at least with two or three others, is a very natural part of daily routine. Even after a long meeting, the real closing remark is usually "Now, let's go eat" rather than "The meeting is adjourned." Korean churches which have more than one thousand members would still offer lunch after the morning worship on Sundays. In fact, they would even run restaurants and coffee shops for the congregation members. Buddhist temples in Bukhansan Mountain or Gwanaksan Mountain also serve lunch to all visitors and although these facilities have religious reasons for providing food to their members, Koreans in general are very willing to serve food to anyone, anywhere and anytime. From weddings to funerals, meals need to be prepared for everyone and the hosts take all cautions and preparations to satisfy the visitors. If there is not enough food for everyone, it is considered to be an embarrassment and quite a problem. The delivery culture is well-illustrated in Korea's free-delivery service through which people order food even when playing billiards or out on picnics at nearby parks. Hence Koreans scold those who skip meals at work by saying "we work to eat..." No matter how phatic these expressions are, there are many layers of cultural significances when Koreans ask others, "Have you eaten yet?"

II

SOCIAL RELATIONSHIP

5 | What is *jeong* that Koreans often talk about?

One of the best words that describe the characteristics of Korean people's interpersonal relationship would be *jeong* which is not an easy word to define or explain in contrast to such a simple one-syllable sound.

People form relationships in many different ways, depending on their cultures and personalities. Each individual also has different types of interpersonal relationship depending on the given situations and persons. In Korea, people often describe their relationship by the amount and degree of *jeong* they have for one another. So what does this *jeong* mean anyway?

Let me give you one example: In Western countries, couples mostly marry for or in the name of love. Korean people, by contrast, often say that they stay in marriage because of *jeong*, not love. In this sense, *jeong* is not love. Rather, it has much more broader meaning than love and sometimes it can even include feelings of hatred. When people stay together through thick and thin, Koreans would say "they must have both affectionate *jeong* and hateful *jeong*." If *jeong* is combined with some negative feelings, it becomes another kind of *jeong*. Moreover, it covers not only one's emotion, which is *jeong-gam* in Korean, but also a rational element called *jeong-ri*. *Jeong-ri* is the combination of ethics and morality that people should consider for interpersonal relationship. Koreans believe that *jeong-gam* is supposed to have derived from *jeong-ri* in interpersonal relationship. To non-Koreans who distinguish and separate contrasting emotions from reasoning, the meaning of *jeong* would be a great challenge to understand.

Another interesting thing about *jeong* is that it is not an intended intimacy. It is impossible to deliberately establish *jeong* with someone. The sense of *jeong* occurs naturally over a long period of time. Koreans consider the relationship, which is built upon *jeong*, as the most resilient and solid unity in which people are no longer distinguish the boundaries between oneself and the other. Needless to say, the best and the easiest way to feel *jeong* for Koreans is through their family members. No other feeling is comparable to *jeong* between parents and children or between brothers and sisters. Being a family means that individual boundaries or privacy no longer exists between the members and they become "we" as one. People also feel family-like attachments and develop *jeong* to those who are not related by blood, meaning that they become very close to each other without any personal boundaries.

When people establish *jeong*, it is hard to break the tie even when they go through bad times or are disappointed with each other. For Koreans, *jeong* is much more of a superior feeling than any other emotions. The most negative comment about one's personality is that he or she is a person who cannot establish or gain *jeong* from others. The person who draws this kind of comments would be someone who has difficulty fitting in to any group of people and tends to build only superficial relationship with others. So who are these people with whom Koreans cannot feel *jeong*? It would be easier to answer such question by looking at the type of people who develop *jeong* easily in interpersonal relationships. A person who is full of *jeong* is likely to be considerate and kind-hearted. Koreans tend to value those who are amicable and modest. In contrast, people generally do not like to interact with those who are arrogant and self-centered and thus difficult to give or receive *jeong*.

Unlike first impressions or instant affections, *jeong* builds up over a long period of time. Some Koreans worry that more and more people have less *jeong* in the modern Korean society, that they are becoming increasingly more individualistic and self-centered. What is then the future of *jeong* that was once the most fundamental emotion in Korean society?

6 | Why is the meaning of "yes" and "no" unclear in Korea?

A foreigner being confused by Korean people's yes and no is a very special yet common phenomenon in Korea. As a result of people's reluctance to openly disclose their feelings, people who come from other cultures where yes and no relatively have a clear and direct meaning can experience difficulties because of such unique characteristic of Koreans. When they say yes, it does not mean either yes or no but rather, yes is no and no is neither no or yes but has a more complex meaning. Koreans usually refer to the outer and inner heart or *keotmaeum* and *sokmaeum*, respectively. Called differently, these two concepts exist almost in every culture. Such mindsets often occur when a person's social or cultural norms versus his social status don't really meet his own demands and motivations. Koreans use the words *keotmaeum* and *sokmaeum* when they want to say that a particular situation or moral obligation requires one's reaction that may differ from his or her true feelings or thoughts. *Chemyeon* (appearance) and *nunchi* (tactfulness) often used in expressions such as to save face or to keep face show that one's social status is very closely linked to his or her appropriate behaviors and hence the expression: Saving face. Regardless one's real intention, it is necessary to behave the way that fits one's social status. The ability to read *keotmaeum* and *sokmaeum* is thus required in order to function effectively and appropriately in Korean society. It is important to differentiate between people's real thoughts and their forced behavior to save face.

Most foreigners may find it difficult to save other's "face." Koreans themselves often find it difficult to read each other's *sokmaeum* so they also misunderstand or misread the situation. Why don't Koreans say what they really mean instead and save a lot of people from miscommunications and misunderstandings? Well, this is why having the ability of *nunchi* is very important in Korea because it enables people to understand other's inner feelings and read between the lines. *Nunchi* is a very important skill to Koreans. Sometimes they say: "Must I really say it out loud for you to understand?" Koreans usually expect others to understand their real thoughts without having to say them out. That is why Koreans say it is necessary to be quick-witted and catch the real meanings behind people's actions and words. Koreans also avoid direct refusals not to hurt other people. When Koreans are put in an uncomfortable situation to choose between the given options, they try to conceal their thoughts as much as they can. Actually, *chemyeon* and *nunchi* are very delicate concepts whose meanings may differ depending on the contexts and situations. They should be considered as unique characteristics of Korean people's way of communication. How should you then act in order to get a clear yes or no from Korean people? Unfortunately, there cannot be one clear answer to such direct questions.

7 | Why do Koreans share their glass with each other while drinking?

A group of doctors from Pohang gathered together to draft a strongly worded resolution. It included some central points about the Korean drinking custom: people should not force drinking to others, share their cups or glasses with others, prohibit bar-hopping, and ban *poktanju* or bomb drinks that is a mixture of various alcohols. These doctors felt compelled to encourage proper drinking culture and could no longer just sit back and watch Koreans ruin their health. The drinking custom, however, requires some understanding of Korean culture first.

In Korea, the annual amount of alcohol consumed by the entire nation and by individuals is by far one of the highest in the world. Korea is the best in the world when it comes to offering drinks to others and constantly going from one bar to another for several rounds of drinking. Although there are no statistics to prove the drinking speed, it would not be surprising if Koreans drink most quickly and rapidly in the shortest amount of time. The main objective of the first "session" is to get drunk as quickly as possible and then offering continuous toasts and one-shots to others. There are other cultures that mix various alcoholic drinks but Korea's *poktanju* is far more creative and exciting.

Just as there are a wide array of different alcoholic drinks, the drinking custom and the cultural meaning of alcohol varies from one nation to another. Koreans think they become closer to others through drinking and likewise, drinking allows us to have a better understanding of one's culture. Foreigners who have had the chance to drink with Koreans are often greatly astonished by the drinking custom that demands one to drink very quickly and share drinks from the same cup.

Since when did Koreans start drinking so quickly and share the same cup with others? Alcohol always performed a number of consequential roles in Korea's ancient history but it is hard to find records about the origin of such custom of drinking from the same cup.

One possibility is that alcohol is the best solution to getting along with others and by sharing the drinking glasses, people form a sense of intimacy and unity. Koreans used to say, "In order to live under the same roof, one needs to share the rice from the same bowl." The drinking custom follows the same principle in that sharing the same glass allows one to create and strengthen the solidarity between individuals and groups. There is a strong belief that drinking with a person you meet for the first time will reduce the psychological distance between the two and that taking turns to drink from the same cup also allows people to become as close as a family. In Korea, where friendship and loyalty are regarded as some of the most important values, drinking is a very essential part of people's social life. Without being able to drink, one cannot even start up a business which in turn has prompted for the so called "drinking employees" who are hired by the CEOs to attend the evening gatherings and drink on their behalf. There is no doubt that such a bizarre occupation exists only in Korea.

The world is constantly changing and now that health is regarded as everyone's number one priority, more and more people are starting to protest against Korea's drinking culture that is in need of at least several alterations. In fact, it is very costly for those who are constantly forced to drink alcohol all night long. With recent studies showing that drinking from the same glass is not only unsanitary but also lead to gastritis and hepatitis, people are becoming increasingly more concerned about Korea's drinking culture. Until recently, a woman suing her boss for forcing her to drink was unthinkable. Will Korea's drinking culture see a change? Will the insanitary practice of drinking from the same cup disappear too?

Unfortunately, the rate of alcohol consumption is still high in Korea and people still share and drink from the same glass despite the various campaigns to reduce alcohol consumption. A dissertation submitted to one of the tourist institutes further examined Korea's *poktanju* culture and asserted that it has at least nine positive impacts. One of them is that *poktanju* allows people to get drunk much faster so that it is the most cost-effective way of creating a sense of harmony and unity between people. And people still share glasses throughout the night.

8 | Why do Koreans call their spouses 'our' husband or 'our' wife?

Saying 'our' husband is not just wrong from a grammatical point of view but it also confuses the listeners. Koreans say it all the time and if a person says 'my husband' or 'my wife,' he or she may seem arrogant to other Koreans. Stressing one's own ownership is considered selfish and uncooperative behavior against collectivism which is an important part of Korean culture that resulted in a uniquely Korean expression called 'we-ism' or *uri*-ism (*uri* means 'we' in Korean). Koreans say our family, our school, our company, our country, which seem like a passionate obsession of collective consciousness that may be worth a cultural research.

Stressing the importance of groups and relationships over an individual has to do with a long history and lifestyle of Koreans. In traditional agricultural Korean society, the collective values were of a great importance. Farmers' cooperative groups and exchange of labor phenomenon emerged in villages where all members were working together for the entire village's prosperity. In agrarian society, a group cooperation wasn't a choice but a mandatory requirement for survival. There were no borders between houses and a village became one family and many villages consisted of the descendants of one ancestor so there was no 'mine' but 'ours' that even included husbands, wives, and children.

Together with agrarian lifestyle, the Confucian ethics also strengthened Korea's tradition of we-ism. Confucian values teaches that more than the individual pursuits, fulfilling one's role as a society member and establishing a harmonious relationship with others are more important. These teachings also play an integral role in strengthening collectivistic values among Koreans.

Koreans who say 'our company' and 'our school' have shared devotion and love with other people as well as a strong nationalism. This collectivism is also believed to be one of the key factors contributing to Korea's fast economic growth. Some believe that such devotion of Korean workers and readiness to sacrifice themselves for their company's benefits, made *chaebol* companies like Samsung and Hyundai some of the major global leaders. Koreans are very much familiar with expressions such as Samsung family or Hyundai family.

On one hand, collectivism is a source of a great power but on the other hand, it can have a negative influence. When Koreans form a close group consisted of 'us' (*uri*), those outside the group automatically become the 'outer groups.' When one belongs to the group, he or she can easily find from it cooperation and sympathy but those outside the group become hostile enemies. Koreans value collectivism inside their groups but they tend to be indifferent and discriminatory toward everyone else outside the group.

Unlike in the past, the components of individualism are gradually integrated into Korea's contemporary culture but Koreans to this day never say 'my home' but 'our home.'

9 | What is *sogae-ting*?

On every Saturday, many cafes and hotel lounges in Korea are crowded with young people on blind dates. The word *sogae-ting* is the term combined of words *sogae* (meaning an introduction in Korean) and *–ting* (a shortened form of an English word 'meeting'). The word *sogae-ting* is equivalent to a blind date but its connotation is not that simple. Many words ending with the letter 'ting' used in Korean usually involve meeting someone and may sound exotic and strange to foreigners. For example, there are words like meet-ting, Sogae-ting, phone-ting, chat-ting, hunt-ting in Korean. Usually, these words are used in connection with interactions between men and women. These kinds of words continually crop up and disappear from time to time. What is the difference between *sogae-ting* and meet-ting? In short, *sogae-ting* is more like a one-to-one blind date. Since *sogae-ting* is arranged by an acquaintance, both a man and a woman tend to treat each other formally and with care. It is also hard to reject the other party easily as in a more casual and informal meet-ting dates. If it is *sogae-ting* between a man and a woman in their marriageable age, it might be more serious and formal like a family-to-family arrangement meeting rather than between two individuals.

"Meet-ting" is like a ceremony into the adulthood for many young college students. In Korean society that has a strict distinction and separation between boys and girls, meet-ting may be almost the first social occasion for young students to formally meet their potential partners. The anticipation and excitement for freshmen when attending a first Meet-ting arranged by the department representative become an unforgettable memory. Coffee shops near colleges are packed with young male and female college students of similar age in a Meet-ting. It is even said that Meet-ting is like a rite of passage for college freshmen before taking any required courses!

When judging from advertisements on a bus or subway these days, Korea looks like a lovers' paradise. Matchmaking agencies are very active and very specialized. Even some TV shows feature matchmaking dates between celebrities.

If you search *sogae-ting* on the internet, you may easily find many contents about how to give a good impression on the first blind date or how to succeed in *sogae-ting*. From people's vivid experiences, you may also learn how to meet the best partners and how to avoid the so-called "bombs," meaning the worst possible dating partner. Numerous advice columns and episodes related to love are on the internet. There are some examples universal advice such as 'show your smile to give a good impression' but international students may find advice like 'if you are a woman, expose your weakness' somewhat confusing. Showing your weakness means not to act too perfect in front of a man. In other words, a woman needs to act imperfect to be attractive because many Korean men do not like or are afraid to date those who seem better than them, too perfect or flawless.

Dating is a universal occurrence but there are unique kinds of meetings between different sexes depending on different cultures and societies.

10 | Why do Korean female students hold hands or link arms with each other when walking together?

There are different norms of physical contact in different cultures. There are places where you can and cannot touch. The part of culture is reflected in human contacts and gestures. One of the most surprising things for foreign students in Korea is that Korean girls walk together holding each other's hands or linking arms together. In Western cultures, such gestures in public are considered to be a sign of homosexuality. In Korea, these gestures are possible even between same sex as a show of affection and friendship. Such different interpretations of the same body gestures are good examples of how different one culture is from another. Linking arms with friends is a show of affection and intimacy between friends. Once they become much closer, they can even slap each other's hips among other physical contacts which may be considered to be indications of homosexuality and cause misunderstandings.

The different meanings in physical contacts become most noticeable when Korean students go abroad, too. In one Canadian weekly magazine there was a feature article about Korean female students folding arms. The closer people get the more they care about communion and in this context, folding arms and other physical contacts even between women or men is considered an expression of friendliness. Korean female students say that first they fold arms when they get close to each other enough to start holding hands. Like this the physical contact is becoming a measure of friendliness and depends on it.

Korea is relatively tolerant to intimate physical contacts between people of the same sex. That is why there are many physical contacts between men, too. Some foreign male students seemed very shocked when their Korean male friends hug them and sit very close to them, touching their thighs or knees in the bars or restaurants. Hearing from other Koreans that these gestures are usually a show of affection and closeness or an attempt to get friendlier is a very relieving knowledge for foreign men who tried to persuade themselves that their Korean friends were merely expressing their kindness and friendliness in a wrong way. Although at first, such physical contacts between people of the same sex may seem shocking to some foreigners but there are many foreign students who are actually envious of such closeness between friends. Nowadays, Koreans use special non-verbal language amongst themselves.

11 | Why don't Koreans knock on the door?

Things have changed a lot these days but Koreans are still very unlikely to knock and wait for an answer. Knocking is merely a formality that has a meaning of its own. So what does the knocking really mean to Koreans? They do not have their own word for knocking so they simply use the Korean pronunciation of the English word and say "*no-k*." The traditional doors in Korea were sliding screens made out of rice papers so it was not possible for Koreans to knock on them to produce a knocking sound. Instead, they would alert their presence to those behind the doors by clearing their throat or by dry coughing. Depending on one's age and social position, the dry coughing sound varied: a child or a subordinate could not use the elder's dry cough sound. A Korean literature scholar once translated the act of "knocking" as hand-coughing.

Nowadays, knocking is a very universal etiquette and sign but the gesture and the number of knocks differ by situations and cultures. In America, it is common to knock three times before entering inside but when ringing a bell, once is enough. However, knocking three times on the bathroom door might give a sense of urgency and may seem very inconsiderate and rude for someone inside. Instead, twice is appropriate. You also knock twice before entering a family member's room. In short, knocking is a basic manner even between close friends and family members in America. In contrast, Koreans treat knocking merely as a gesture of formality and although they observe the usual etiquettes in their first visit, they would walk in and out of their friend's house as if it is their own once they become close to each other.

The space layout of the traditional Korean houses is another reason why Koreans' knocking culture is different from other countries. The open structure of the traditional Korean houses has a shared gardens and floors between rooms and different wings, very unlike the Western-style house that has rooms along the narrow aisle. Also, Koreans usually keep their windows open. When someone in the family gets angry, the first thing he or she does is to shut the door as a way to refuse any communication and show a desire to be alone. In this way, knocking becomes a sign between a person inside and a person outside, a sign of distance between persons. Eventually, an act of knocking between family members, friends, or colleagues at work became less frequent and turned into a mere gesture of formality and thus entering immediately after knocking without waiting for an answer may be understood as Koreans' way of showing closeness and intimacy rather than drawing a line between private and public spaces.

12 | Why do Koreans prepare an enormous amount of food and tell their guests to eat more?

The most common and the best way to treat people in Korea is to offer them food. When Koreans meet with an old or a new friend, they usually say: "Let's have dinner soon" and bid good bye. When Koreans invite friends or co-workers to their houses, a meal is a must. People show their best good will to a person inviting him home and serving home-made food. Inviting people home and preparing food, however, takes up a lot of time and energy so dining out is becoming a much more common practice nowadays. They build friendship and discuss business while sharing a meal together. This is one of the most common social activities in Korea and thus Seoul boasts the highest density of restaurants in the world.

On some occasions, the guests must be invited home. In such situations Koreans usually prepare a lot of food and say, "Please enjoy even though we haven't prepared much." Most foreigners would feel a little strange hearing this when a feast has been prepared for them. Traditional Korean restaurants show a similar attitude as they offer unlimited refills of side dishes even when there are a lot of other choices. Koreans tell their guests to eat more and more even when they are eating a lot and quite full.

Of course, in a real situation, it is impossible to eat all the time without a break. When Koreans say "there is not much," they are trying to be modest and when they urge their guests to eat more, they are trying to assure them that there is no need to worry about food. Not too long ago, Korea was a very poor country. The whole country was devastated by the Korean War (1950-1953) and people suffered from food shortage. The parents and grandparents of today's university students remember those times very clearly. Because there was a lack of rice and other natural resources, the hunger was one of the major problems for Korean people and treating guests with food was a privilege and highly regarded. Except the ruling class, almost everyone suffered from a food shortage but still tried to treat their guests who were also aware of the situation. Their hosts insisted their guest to eat more and not to worry about the food themselves. In this way, the act of sharing food together symbolized generosity, hospitality and the beginning of a warm relationship between the guests and hosts. There is plenty of food to go around these days but Koreans still follow the old habit and continue to urge their guests to eat more.

III
KOREANS

13 | Why do Koreans seem quiet and reticent?

Foreigners often think that Koreans look cold or even angry. Are Koreans really cold? Or do they just look like that but are actually friendly and talkative? Of course, the measure of kindness and friendliness is very subjective but it really seems that Koreans' facial expression tend to be on the stiff side in general. It is definitely not the abnormal facial muscles so we should try to find a cultural reason behind that.

There may be several reasons why Koreans look cold or even angry. The first reason is the influence of Confucianism. Being able to control one's own emotions was an important part of becoming *seonbi*,[1] or Confucian scholar, and was accepted as a duty in older times. Showing real emotions was considered shameful and was a mark of immaturity and insufficient self-cultivation. Some Korean customs followed this Confucian tradition and boys are taught from an early age that they must not cry and brides must not laugh or smile during the wedding ceremonies lest that they have bear a daughter as a result of their uncultivated behavior—Although less so nowadays, there was a strong preference of sons over daughters in the old days.

The second reason is connected with rapid modernization and the Korean War during which many people died and struggled for survival. A famous Korean habit of *"ppalli ppalli"* resulted from postwar Korean society's attempt to reach the level of Japan and other advanced countries on a state level, and show off their own success and superiority over other cultures on a personal level. With such determination, the smile on a face was considered hypocritical and lazy. It is not easy to see a relaxed or

1
Seonbi is a person who is in the pursuit of learning without having any official position of the government. It usually refers a person who is educated and noble.

smiling expression on the faces of Koreans who have worked hard to overcome the devastating consequences of the Korean War. Constant competitions with other countries and other people led Koreans to live under pressure. Such living conditions make it impossible to keep relaxed or maintain a smile on their faces.

Now we can understand that Korean people's expression is not non-talkativeness or unfriendliness but rather a result of living under constant pressure to overcome the difficult period. The facial expressions of the famous Hahoe masks (masks used during mask dance in Hahoe village) have special meanings. During the Joseon dynasty, the class system was largely divided into three: the *yangban* (upper class), commoners, and slaves. The masks that represented *yangban* usually wore very serious expressions while those of the commoners had laughing expressions. The performers mocked and ridiculed such hypocrisy and seriousness of *yangban* in mask dance. The lower class, however, didn't have any power but only anger towards the monarch system, and the masks representing them had laughing expressions. These traditional masks and their expressions reflect historical and cultural history of Korea. How will the facial expressions of Koreans change in the future?

14 | Why are Korean people so reluctant to wait in line?

Here is an interesting anecdote about Koreans' attitude toward waiting in line. The story takes place in Moscow: There was a long line of people waiting in line to get a table in a famous Moscow restaurant. Three people, one from China, Japan, and Korea, were also waiting in line but they had different ideas about the situation:

Chinese : These people are lined up so neatly that they must be very honest.

Japanese : There are so many people waiting in line to eat at the restaurant so it must be the most famous in town or have some delicious and special dishes!

Korean : The restaurant owner should feel bad about making the customers wait so long instead of planning in advance to avoid such a delay.

It would be silly to find out whether or not this anecdote is true. In fact, someone might have made it up to emphasize different cultural characteristics between nations. Regardless, the anecdote about people's different attitude toward waiting in line offers intriguing cultural and social implications.

Actually, many foreigners think Koreans are hot-tempered and impatient wherever they are. Does this mean that Koreans really dislike waiting in line? What could possibly make them so impatient? Before we explore these questions, let me talk a little bit about the act of waiting in line itself.

Waiting in line to wait for one's turn is a practice that developed in the modern era and traditionally it referred to a procession of people with authority and power. In other words, people in the modern era try to keep social order and wait for their turn because they know it is efficient and rational to do so. After all keeping order protects everyone from a state of chaos and disorder. Waiting in line has been taken for granted but it stems from the central principle that all people are born equal. Such a custom would have been impossible in the past when there were class and social stratification. Commoners and slaves had to yield everything to the nobles. A modern society promised everyone an equal opportunity, equal rights, and responsibilities. There are still some people who don't abide by the social order or who don't need to wait in line because of their social power even with the modern education system that teaches people the social rules such as waiting in line. For example, the first thing you learn when entering elementary school is standing in line. Queuing ensures everyone that each would all get his or her turn but at the same time, it also effectively controls numerous issues in this modern civilization where lots of different people live together. In this light, the different process of modern civilization as well as different experiences of social order and regulations may have resulted in people's different attitude about the practice of waiting in line. Voluntary and effective queuing is related to a more enhanced sense of citizenship and social customs. We should not make a simplistic judgment about people's different attitudes when waiting in line.

A relatively yet greatly different queuing culture in Japan left a deep impression on many Koreans in recent years. Particularly, it was very moving to see how people kept order in and stood in line during the great Hanshin earthquake and at the places of refuge afterwards. To Japanese people, Korean's disorderly behavior when waiting in line may seem impolite and even uncivilized. Koreans do stand in line: just like Japanese, they stand in three fork-shaped lines in spacious places such as a subway or train stations. Waiting in line for their turn is becoming very important to Koreans, and as a result the ticket dispenser machines are rapidly increasing to shorten the wait-time for those standing in line.

However, many Koreans still prefer to get quick and instant

services. Quite a number of people now pay a lot of money to hire a substitute who could wait in line on their behalf so that they could get what they want without having to wait in line. If you see a store with many Korean people in line, you should check it out. The place must be terrific for impatient and quick-tempered Koreans to invest their time and wait so patiently!

15 | Why do Korean women care so much about their appearance?

Even Korean men care about their appearances a lot. The so-called "pin-up boy" syndrome shows that men's appearances affect their job opportunities as well as a better life style. Who doesn't like handsome and pretty people anyway? It is very natural to desire beauty and everyone probably wants to be handsome or pretty. The obsession with appearances in Korea, however, has gone beyond such natural desire and is becoming a social problem. Seven out of ten Korean women are stressed out because of their appearances and even high school students try to get a plastic surgery to improve their looks before they start college. It is not just a matter of becoming more attractive but is a reflection of a serious social problem. The so called "lookism" which prioritizes one's appearance more than his or her personality and talents is widespread in Korea. As a result, the beauty treatment and plastic surgery industries are expanding very rapidly every day so much so that some hospitals offer a "plastic surgery reception" that provides a speedy, reliable plastic surgery service for foreign clients. Various advertisements for skin laser services, plastic surgeries, as well as diet programs can be found all over the country.

Lookism seems to be related to personal desire but in fact, it is a very hierarchical and sexual phenomenon. What are the standards of beauty then? A well-shaped body, an egg-shaped face, big eyes, pale skin, a long and thin nose are all dependent upon the money and time one can afford to invest in his or her appearance. In other words, one's looks nowadays have a direction relationship to one's economic capital and wealth. Moreover, the lookism is a sexual phenomenon. Although Korean men are no exception to the lookism, they are less affected by it than Korean women. A clean-cut and neat and tidy appearance was the most important asset for women on the job market but now they are replaced by their faces. The legal system has brought about many changes to prevent such lookism but one's appearance is still a significant factor in society. According to one of the wedding consulting agency, the key factor for a good husband is his career whereas for a good bride, it is her appearance. Korea's lookism is a social violence prevalent in Korean society and it is dividing everyone and everything into beauty or ugly, masculine or feminine, normal or abnormal. When fashion industry keeps producing clothes that do not actually fit average body size and shape, it is violating people's right to choose their own size and look the way they do but forcing them to mold themselves to the fashion industry's standard. In today's society, having a potbelly means laziness a pair of short legs bad genes and poor working class. The society is molding people to fit themselves into a unified and standardized beauty. Before it is too late for us, we have to ask ourselves where such lookism came from. The visual media including TV, movies, and signboards on the streets are overwhelming and they are influencing people to desire an immediate stimulus which in turn cause them to become more and more violent.

16 | Why do Korean women wear strong and vivid colors?

Many foreigners, especially those from Japan, ask this question a lot. But we should be careful not to generalize because Chinese and Japanese people also like bright and vivid colors on some occasions. So let us explore when Korean people prefer to use a certain color for which occasions. It is a well-known fact that Chinese people prefer the color red and Japanese women like to wear Kimonos with splendid colors in order to give other people a strong impression. A lot of researchers are greatly interested in color preference and color sense in different cultures.

It can be relatively simple to answer why Korean women wear more vivid colors compared to Japanese women who prefer neutral hues. Most Koreans choose colors to express their individuality and sometimes to show themselves off to others. Interestingly enough, Koreans' way of self-assertion cannot be solely explained through colors only. The most popular automobile colors in Korea are achromatic colors such as black, grey, silver, and white. Traditional meaning of black is authoritative and powerful as previously discussed so for the larger vehicles, black is more popular than other colors. It hasn't been that long since the color black became a symbol of authority. It is not irrelevant that Koreans who experienced the Japanese occupation period associate the color black with the Japanese authority and military policemen in black uniforms.

These days, it's not difficult to find the streets of Seoul filled with numerous colors of cars unlike in the past. More and more cars in vivid colors such as yellow and red are increasing especially among the younger generations with compact cars. People seem to express themselves differently depending on their age and social status. Regardless of people's preference for different colors, they are all similar and what they want in the end is to assert themselves to others. However, the trend of bright and vivid colors in Korea is a fairly recent phenomenon.

The Joseon dynasty was greatly influenced by Confucianism. Confucianism values the inner spirit rather than extravagant or loud exterior so people in general preferred white, which could hardly be considered a color. Koreans were called the 'white-clad race' because almost the entire population wore only white clothes and even made white porcelain. Although they worshipped white, they also used vivid colors on some occasions during the Joseon period. The five cardinal colors – blue, black, red, white, and yellow – were used on girl's jackets with sleeves in multi-colored stripes and many other ceremonial dresses.

The major five natural elements are based on the principles of the negative and positive (Yin and Yang) energies that can also be represented by the five cardinal colors. Many Koreans believed that blessings would come your way if you pursue your life following the five elements of Yin and Yang but if you don't, you would encounter a great misfortune in your life. This idea enormously influenced Koreans' sense of color. We can also find this color principle in traditional houses decorated with multicolored artworks. Today, we can see a similar colorful rainbow-striped pattern on the tail wings of Asiana airplanes, one of the airline companies in Korea.

Koreans' color sense underwent a lot of changes loosing its traditional elements. Due to the rapidly developing fashion industry, various designs have been imported from abroad and neutral colors as well as primary colors quickly spread throughout the nation. A number of products from all over the world including Japan, USA, and European countries are now sold in Korea and people now purchase dark colors that were once taboo in Korea. Perhaps in several decades, Koreans' favorite color might change again.

17 | Why do Korean women smoke in the toilet?

We become interested in other cultures' small and trivial things first. Many exchange students, especially female students, often ask why Korean women smoke in the bathrooms that seems so inconvenient. Do the cigarettes taste better when smoked in an enclosed space? Such a trifle behavior actually provides a window to a very strict cultural and social implication.

Although there aren't any legal regulations to prohibit Korean women from smoking on the street, they face more direct and severe social consequences that outweigh the law. It is kind of a social taboo for Korean women to smoke in public spaces and when they do, they have to endure prejudices, verbal abuse, or even at times, physical violence. A simple act of smoking on the streets for Korean women requires courage and a spirit of resistance. Rather than facing such complications, they just choose to find their own private space, such as bathrooms, where they can smoke freely without worrying about others' scrutiny. Negative perspectives towards smoking women stem from the idea that women are mothers: they give birth to children and nurture them. Thus, smoking which threatens their body as a future mother is considered careless, selfish, and unethical.

More than the relationship between smoking and health, the socio-cultural and socio-psychological reasons that drive these women to smoke in secret. There are many other countries that treat women's smoking as a social taboo. Especially in a patriarchal society, smoking is men's exclusive right not allowed to women. In this context, women's smoking is not regarded as just a preference but a code of resistance to the patriarchal society.

Cigarette retailers once used this image of resistance as a marketing strategy and thus the image of a successful career women smoking gained a lot of popularity. People began to fantasize about intelligent, sexy, and sophisticated career women holding a cigarette in their slender fingers. Unlike the declining number of male smokers world-wide, the number of female smokers is on the rise, especially in Asian countries. The importance of quitting smoking is emphasized by the media and people almost every day; but for Korean women, smoking is related to their cultural rights and protest against patriarchal society. How long will it take for Korean women to quit smoking in the bathrooms?

18 | Who is *ajumma*?

The actual meaning of aunt, *ajumma*, is almost opposite to its meaning in the dictionary. *Ajumma* in a dictionary is a friendly term referring to a "middle-aged woman." But in reality, everyone wants to avoid being called as such so much so that people prefer to be called as *unni* (an elder sister) or *imo* (a maternal aunt) instead of *ajumma* especially in the service industries. So who is this *ajumma* in Korea then?

Ajumma in Korea has a very strong stereotypical image of a vulgar, ignorant, old-fashioned, and immodest middle-aged woman. They are self-centered and loud women who have lost their femininity or any feminine characteristics. Speaking loudly in public, running desperately to grab a vacant seat in the subway or on the bus, they speculate in land properties and horde all necessities just for themselves and their families without any consideration for others.

Married women who have not become grandmothers are generally categorized as *ajumma*. This makes one fifth of the total population in Korea, which is about 10 million people, *ajumma*. The common negative perception about *ajumma* has inspired much academic research and discourses on Korea's married or middle-aged women, as well as "*ajumma* rights movements." A feminist scholar, Lee Sook-kyeong initiated the "Bill of Rights for *ajumma*" with 20 provisions. The most essential ones are as follows : 1. We are first mothers ; 2. We are first daughters-in-law ; 3. We are first wives ; 4. We are first human beings.

The denouncements and unfair stereotypes of *ajumma* are almost like group bullying but are nonetheless one of the unique features of Korean society. A character in a Korean movie even says, "there are three genders in the world and that is, a male, female, and *ajumma*." *Ajumma*, in short, is a genderless and unique social person.

During the modernization process and under patriarchal Korean society, *ajumma* has been forced to set herself aside as an independent individual but take the responsibilities and obligations as a wife, mother, as well as a daughter-in-law. *Ajumma*, in many ways, have become victims of the most unfair and rigid oppressions from the society. It is thus important for us to acknowledge their responsibilities and obligations as wives and mothers. Most *ajumma* are the ones who provide most of the labors at home without getting any reward. Only sacrifice is demanded and required from them. If the price of one's life sacrifice is this kitsch and genderless image of an *ajumma*, they are the most miserable group of people in the world. Married women in Korea have obtained the proper noun *ajumma* and forged a bizarre pact among themselves that they would become the last warriors of the family and the nation in crisis. Nevertheless, this kind of praise also asks for *ajumma* to deny their individual identity. Who made these women '*ajumma*' anyway?

19 | Why do Korean men like to be called *oppa*?

Let us look at the word *oppa* which means an 'elder brother' in Korean. The word literally means a friendly term for a female member's blood-related older male brother. In Korea, however, it is likely to be used by a woman calling a man who is older than her even when they are not related to each other. Some foreigners feel awkward when Korean women introduce their spouses as their *oppa*.

Jo Yong-pil, one of the most famous musicians in Korea, is now over 60-years old. Regardless of his biological age, his fans still call him an "everlasting *oppa*." The word expresses friendly and affectionate feelings toward the addresser. When *oppa*'s fans get large in number, they form a fandom of *oppa* that is called the "*oppa*-troop." Even today, there are fans of Jo who now have grandchildren but still call him *oppa* at his concerts. What is interesting is that this word does not only belong to Jo or to any specific individuals but is widely used when women of all ages call older men.

Why do Korean men like to be called *oppa*? We need to understand the cultural context beyond its implication of kinship to answer this question. The word is closely related to what Korean men want and how they identify themselves. The term *oppa* implies the obligations and rights that an elder brother should take care of his younger sisters. Thus, being called *oppa* clarifies the relationship that he is situated in the higher position than his younger sister who is weaker and should be protected. Being someone's *oppa* means that he has a duty to take care of his sister but at the same time, it is the acknowledgement of his authority and power as well as the woman's respect towards him. In this sense, it is understandable that Korean men feel good and grin as if they are disarmed when some women called them *oppa*. That is why the Korea's service industry is using this psychology of Korean men and calling male customers *oppa* instead of *ajeossi* (meaning adult man).

In short, the term *oppa* is often used strategically by a woman who wants to establish the special relationship that is entailed in using the term with a man. If a female student calls an upper class male student as *hyeong*, which is another informal word for an older brother but only used by a younger male, she is choosing to exclude her femininity and gender in their relationship. It is also a very interesting parallel that a male salesperson calls a female customer *unni*, a term addressing an elder female by a younger female.

20 | Don't Korean men need to serve the military when the two Koreas unify?

Nonsense! Regardless of the reunification issue, military service will remain mandatory for all men for the national security and welfare of the reunited nation. We may even need a much larger scale of army then. The real question is whether or not the state will abolish the conscription policy and implement voluntary service instead. To ask "Do we have to serve in the army?" is to hope for the voluntary service.

Military duty is a very sensitive issue for Koreans since military duty has been considered as an honor. Those who regard military service as a duty are not limited to just men who actually serve in the army for about two years but includes everyone else who have to be separated from their sons, brothers, cousins, boyfriends, and etc. Accordingly, the military duty feels like such a normal part of Korean people's daily lives that they rarely question or the thought of questioning the duty don't even dawn on them at all. "Can I avoid the military service?" A desire to avoid the military service is like trying to weasel out of the patriotic responsibility to protect the nation and to lose the chance to become a real man. Koreans say, "You won't be a real man unless you go to the army."

While the military service seems like a natural part of life, however, there are always men who try to dodge the draft; some even make a career out of devising a way to avoid the military service and they have quite a lot of clients requesting their service. Not surprisingly enough, these men illegally skipping the military service are at the risk of stirring social outcry should others ever find out about them. If people ever find out that a politician pulled some strings to spare his son from the military duty, his political career would be over. I cannot stress enough that the military duty is one of the most sensitive and quite "explosive" issues in Korea.

It's been more than 50 years since South Korea initiated the military conscription. To be exact, the military service law was established in 1949 by the first South Korean President Lee Seung-man (Syngman Rhee) and its basis, though with several amendments, has been maintained since then. Particularly, Park Jeong-hee (Park Chung-hee)'s regime further reinforced the image of great soldiers protecting the nation. The military service has become a collective conviction relying on the sacrifice of Korean men and their fathers, mothers, sisters, and wives. The experience of Japanese imperialism and the Korean War required every Korean man to serve in the army without any excuse. President Park Jeong-hee's Korea was no different from a garrison state, equipped with hundreds of thousand regular armed forces and even local reserve army units. All Korean men regardless of their education or social background must serve in either the regular or reserve army.

The irony was that the government or state could still control such an absolute "divine" duty. The culture built upon the sacrifices of the individuals was threatening the basic human rights of Korean men and women. Isn't the divine duty equivalent to the infringement of individual rights during the military training? Can we justify the life of those soldiers who perish in the army as a divine sacrifice? In every nook and corner of the nation lay the inflexible authority and mentality of the army. Accordingly, the collective experiences that all Korean men share through their years spent in the military service form a strong tie between them and those few who did not serve in the army for one reason or another become an outcast. In a way, the military service experiences remain everywhere even after Korean men complete their service. Endless anecdotes and episodes about their times in the army are always a hot topic for men although any doubts or questions about the mandatory military service is still a social taboo in Korea.

21 | What age does one become a grandfather or a grandmother?

Koreans call someone 'grandpa' or 'grandma' if he or she is over sixty and has at least one grandchild. Koreans throw a large banquet on the sixtieth birthday because it marks a turning point in one's life. The number "sixty" means a completion of a single life cycle. It is actually related to the concept of ten heavenly stems and twelve earthly branches that were previously discussed in relation to the Chinese zodiac signs. Besides such a complicated concept, anyone who lived long enough to celebrate the sixtieth birthday deserved a huge banquet since the past average life span in Korea was much shorter than today.

These days, however, the person who has turned sixty is still considered to be young especially since many of them have unmarried sons and daughters. Therefore, it is a very subtle and sensitive issue to call someone grandpa or grandma especially since not many want to be called as such. With the increase in the average life span of Koreans, particularly Korean women whose average life span is over eighty, many older people feel it is quite unfair to be called grandpa or grandma at the age of sixty. As a result, less and less people celebrate the sixtieth birthday and don't even tell others about it since they think it is no longer something to be celebrated.

Influenced by the Confucian culture, the kinship was very strongly emphasized in Korea and it further complicated the ways of addressing others. Koreans call father's male siblings differently based on their ages. For example, you would call your father's elder brother a big uncle or *keunabeoji* and the younger brother a little uncle or *jageunabeoji*. Your father's female siblings would be called *gomo* and your mom's female siblings *imo*.

Aside from the complicating kinship relationships, it is just as difficult to choose appropriate titles for strangers. For example, suppose you meet a woman on the street. You can either call her *unni* (older sister), *agassi* (miss), *ajumma* (mrs.), *ajumeoni* (a politer form of mrs.), *imo* (auntie from mom's side), and so on. Of course, you need to consider the woman's various factors such as her age and social status as well as your own age, gender, and social status. Calling a middle-aged man *ajeossi* (uncle) in Korea assumes that he is a married man. At the same time, it is natural for young students to call their high school male students or unmarried male college students *ajeossi*.

So how do we determine which one of the many labels is appropriate to address the other person? If Japanese people are not sure how to address the other person, they simply say "*sumimasen*" and have no reason to be anxious. Similarly in Korea, many also say, "excuse me" or "*jeogiyo*," when unsure about how to address someone. In order to know the accurate way of addressing someone, you need to fully understand the cultural and social protocols because there are a lot of subtle yet significant differences between each labels. You cannot learn these from textbooks since the distinctions between each labels are very subtle and full of cultural references.

Koreans mostly prefer to be called imo than *ajumma* and Samchon than Ajeossi. Basically, they dislike the terms like *ajumma* or *ajeossi* that make them feel old but most would rather be called imo or samchon to feel closer to the person. Some Koreans even call the female salespersons *imo* and males as *samchon* to build a close relationship with them and receive a better service. Generally, young men are more likely to be called *oppa*, or an older brother, and young women *nuna*, or an older sister. This doesn't mean that *ajeossi* has a negative connotation. In fact, *ajeossi* is considered to be someone who is more considerate and patient compared to a young *oppa*. In this respect, *ajeossi* actually has a better nuance than *oppa*.

Among those who are from the same culture naturally understand the proper way of addressing other people without having to figure out or learn them. They just know when to call someone *oppa* or *ajeossi*. Possibly because of such complex system of addressing other people, most department stores in Korea do not call their customers as *unni, imo, oppa,* or *ajeossi.* They simply choose a neutral and safer terms like "dear customer." Calling someone *unni* or *imo* feels more friendly and personal than call them "dear customer." This is probably why both merchants and customers in traditional or flea markets still call each other *unni, imo, oppa,* or *samchon*!

22 | Why do Koreans seem to prefer squatting over sitting even outside their homes?

To Westerners, Koreans' squat-sitting pose may seem strange. Why would Koreans squat? If you travel to rural areas, you will commonly see people squatting around at bus stops and on the street. Those working in the market places also spend many hours squatting on the ground to sell their goods.

The Korean habit of squatting may be traced back to the old days when they conducted their living on the floors. Relying on the very effective floor heating system called *ondol*, people sat on the floor to eat, study, and sleep. *Ondol* heating system was invented to survive the cold winter days and led to the kind of lifestyle which involved sitting on the floor for most daily tasks. Even though Korean lifestyle has changed a lot like to that of the West, the *ondol* system still continues to influence Koreans' daily life and modern Korean apartments also use floor heating systems. Korean people are so used to sitting on the floor that they still draw their legs up on the chair as if they are sitting on the floor.

The design of Korea's traditional outfit called *hanbok* also reflects the traditional lifestyle setting with as it has a very wide trousers or skirt to accommodate sitting on the floor. If you try sitting on the floor in skinny jeans, you will easily notice how closely clothes and lifestyle are connected to each other.

Sitting on the floor and squatting is definitely different but for Koreans who are used to sitting on the floor, squatting is not a difficult thing to do. They adapted to squatting in order to avoid sitting on the dirty ground. An interesting poll also confirmed that it is more effective to relieve oneself in a traditional toilet that requires one to squat on the floor instead of a sit-down Western style toilet. However, more and more Korean people prefer not to squat on the floor, like those foreigners who find sitting on the floor very uncomfortable and tiring. That is why many public toilets are now equipped with Western style like lavatories rather than the traditional squat-style ones.

Also, the squatting posture is now associated with punishments like "goose walking" (walking while squatting) and known as the main cause of knee joint problems. Increasingly more Koreans are adopting Western life style like sitting on a chair and sleeping on a bed. Perhaps one day, the squatting pose may completely disappear from the Korean lifestyle.

23 | Why do Koreans fight for the bill in restaurants?

It is very common to see Koreans fighting for the bill at a restaurant cash desk. It might look like a noisy quarrel and a trivial matter to most foreigners but paying a bill is a very important matter based on cultural norms for Koreans.

When several people are eating out together, there are two ways to pay a bill. The first method is to pay separately whereas the second method is for one person to pay for everyone. Any arguing or fighting over who is going to pay the bill can be avoided if it is determined before the meal. They begin fighting for the bill when it is not decided in advance. In Korea, there are different ways of saying "to pay separately." One of them is an English expression: Going Dutch. These days, Dutch pay is becoming more common to ease the financial burden of everyone. After *hoesik*, or group meals with co-workers, fighting for the bill is a common occurrence. In order to understand such a cultural norm, it is necessary to first discuss the significance of paying for food in Korea.

Koreans usually think that Dutch pay is a very stingy and cold-hearted way of paying a bill, thinking only of oneself and lacking *inganmi*, or humanity. Paying for others' meal is considered to be a generous act of Inganmi. Some texts introducing an "art of successful living" state one should "become a person who buys meals for others." In other words "a person who buys meals for others" is regarded as someone who cares about others and tries to build a relationship with them. By offering to pay for meals, a person shows his kindness and good will toward others. Such a generous act can also increase one's own social status. And when he encounters some difficulties on the way, he would expect to receive support from others the same way he gave them. In this context, it is understandable why everyone in Korea fight amongst each other to pay first; it is an effective method of earning people's respect. It is not really important who ultimately ends up paying the bill but rather that everyone tries to get involved in the argument instead of just sitting around and looking selfish. A person who does not get involved and just waits around for others to take care of the bill will become a black sheep and hence the reason why Koreans insist on paying for others. Such cultural norms might be difficult for foreigners to understand but an important custom in Korean society.

24 | Why do Koreans feel uncomfortable eating out alone?

These days the number of Koreans eating out alone is rapidly increasing. According to different statistics, there are more and more people who live alone and more restaurants to accommodate such people. Regardless, it is true that most Koreans would feel awkward and uncomfortable eating out by themselves. If we compare Koreans with Japanese, who enjoy eating out alone, we will find some peculiarities in Korea's food culture.

A person who eats alone in a restaurant seems weird and lonely to other Koreans. Even eating alone at home is not a desirable situation. This happens because of Koreans' cultural mentality that avoids any action performed alone. If you tell someone you went to a movie theater by yourself last night, people would think you are strange and may need some help. It doesn't matter whether it is a personal preference or inevitable circumstance; if someone does something alone he or she will be perceived by others as socially awkward and an outcast.

Koreans often eat together from the same plate and drink alcohol by passing around one glass to each other. These traditions go back to an agrarian society when a sense of community was very strong. People always shared food together, even with the dead while performing ancestral worship ceremony or *jesa*. As a result of these traditions, eating alone became a kind of social taboo. After *jesa*, all family members gathered around and shared the sacred food with each other. Consuming food which was believed to be eaten by the deceased ancestors' spirits is called *eumbok*. The deeper and cultural significance of *eumbok* is that sharing food together with others provides essential supplements to both physical and spiritual life so eating in the old days was more than just a physical necessity or pleasure. Because of these past traditions, a person who eats alone becomes an outcast and a stranger from the group. In fact, the basic meal portion in Korean restaurants is usually prepared for two people. It is also difficult to find restaurants designed to accommodate and welcome single diners.

As mentioned earlier, however, there are more and more people who have to or want to eat alone so it is likely to change restaurant seating and menu in the future. For now, seeing Koreans in fast food restaurants gathering all of the French fries onto one plate to share with others assures me that it will take a while for the practice of eating out alone to become a norm in Korea.

25 | Why do Koreans rarely apologize when they bump into each other on the street?

In other countries, when people bump into each other on the street, they usually apologize and say "I'm sorry," "*duìbùqǐ*", "*sumimasen*." In Korea, people usually just walk away without saying anything and act as if nothing had happened. Do they think it is not necessary to apologize or they know they did wrong but don't want to apologize? Is there any other reason for this?

Actually, when Koreans bump into each other, they don't just pass by. Usually, they say something like "ah!" or "oh!" The meaning is not clear enough and is not really an official apology but not an expression of total ignorance either. "Oh!" can be considered as "I accidently bumped into you without an intention but you are at fault, too." Bumping into each other usually happens in the crowded street or market. The streets are too narrow and there are too many people; Koreans are used to such density and don't feel the need to say "I'm sorry" to anyone. Nowadays Koreans simply accept that bumping into others is just an inevitable part of city life and thus they walk away without paying too much attention. Maybe Koreans got used to behaving like this since the Korean War (1950-1953) when everyone struggled for survival, so they are always rushing to get in line or seats first in the subway. What other reasons can there be? Perhaps people have no interest or sympathy for strangers on the streets. Koreans tend to divide others into either 'we (*uri*)' or 'strangers (*nam*).' If Koreans don't feel a special connection with the other person, they tend to just ignore him or her. Random people on the street are the best example of strangers or *nam*. It seems that Koreans don't feel any necessity to show interest, care, or apologize and understand those who have nothing to do with themselves.

IV
STUDY & WORK

26 | Why do high school seniors have dinner at their schools?

If there are foreigners who wonder why high school seniors in Korea have dinner at their schools, then they are becoming aware of the biggest tragedy in modern Korea. Just a quick look at the students' timetables would make anyone understand why they have dinner at schools. Nowhere else would you find such timetables that begin from class Zero which refers to a study session which begins an hour before the official classes begin. Then they have to finish twelve more classes. Korean students spend long hours in school so they definitely need at least one more extra lunch box in addition to the meals provided by schools so that they can study until late for their college entrance examinations. After school, those who have private lessons or examination prep sessions grab instant noodles from the convenient stores to ease their hunger and to stay awake.

Korea is famous for its education zeal and cruel competition among students in order to be accepted by a good university. Success in life is more or less determined by their college degree from a famous university. It also fulfills their first level of filial duty to their parents and brings prestige to the entire family members and relatives. Students who fail to get admittance to any decent universities become not just people who cannot study but also those who are not good to their parents and thus embarrass the family. Korean students study in order to get admitted to universities and not to study. This is the sad truth in Korea. Mathematics, science, foreign languages… such subjects exist in schools all over the world but subjects like *yaja* or *juja* exist only in Korea. *yaja* means an evening studying and *juja* means an afternoon studying. Even when regular classes are over, Korean students still stay in school and study. Nowadays, students go to school only five times a week but most of them ending up going to school on Saturdays to study.

Most Koreans know the expression: "If you sleep for four hours, you will pass an exam but if you sleep for five hours, you will fail." In other words, "If you sleep for more than four hours, you cannot get into a college." Such expression describes a horrible situation which most high school seniors face in Korea. When they eat, they study mathematical formulas, when they walk they study vocabulary and Chinese characters. They study even when they wait for traffic lights or while taking an elevator.

In this vital competition not only students themselves but also their families take an active part. Mothers particularly play an important role in this competition. They have to wake up even earlier than their children to prepare breakfast, then they wait until their children are done with their *yaja* time and return home. After a few hours of sleep, the mothers have to wake up their kids early in the morning. It is not enough if moms take care only of their children's health. They should collect information about academics and private tutoring classes and the best universities for their children. Fathers also work hard to support their children and to provide enormous capital for all private tutoring. Families with high school seniors work more like a team in order to achieve the common goal of sending their seniors to college. Parents of such students are exempted from their social duties. It is all right if parents of high school seniors don't visit wedding ceremonies or funerals. Nobody has a right to accuse them because an entrance into a university is considered the utmost important duty for the parents and family members. After students survive the fight for the university admittance, however, none of them study that hard anymore. Like I mentioned earlier, they simply study to get into a college and to not have to study as hard again.

When will high school students return home early and have conversations with their families over dinner? Such prospects are still gloomy.

27 | Why are Korean parents so obsessed with their child's education?

Though at first the term "obsessed" might seem a little too exaggerated, we would quickly realize that it is actually very true if we closely examine the education of children in Korea today. Every statistic in the world proves that Korean parents have the world's strongest fervor for education. Even among wealthy OECD nations, Korea boasts of the highest levels of education expenses: the private education expenses are even higher than Japan, which also has a renowned fervor for education.

Korea is full of the so-called *gireogi*, or goose, fathers who stay in Korea alone to earn money while his wife and children live abroad to get a better education. Korean mothers who are overzealous about their children's education are called "Gangnam mothers" who are willing to do everything in their power to provide the very best education for their children. So many people's overt commitment to their children's education led to various tragedies such as sudden heart failures, depression, and sometimes even suicides. Gireogi fathers and stressed students are constantly under pressure by the high educational fervor which has become the greatest tragedy and structural imbalance in contemporary Korean society.

The fact that education is still valued today testifies to the prevalence of Confucian values that still yield influence on people today. However, Confucian tradition only partly explains Korea's educational fervor so we need to take other appropriate measures to better understand and reexamine Korea's obsession with education. Education was very important in the Joseon dynasty but it pertained to *yangban* or elite class but in today's class, it seems to be the only goal in life for most young generations as their parents regardless of who or what they are.

Many argue that the current education fervor emerged after the fall of the Joseon dynasty and when Korea was devastated and destabilized by the Japanese annexation and the Korean War. At the time, one's future prospects became very closely tied to one's education that became a new means for social upward mobility. If education in the past was an exclusive privilege to the upper class or to those who could afford it, today's education became available to everyone and through it, they gained the most important social and economic values. Education's universal value is determined by the excessive competition to gain admission to the world's most prestige universities. One's entire life depended upon whether or not he can pass such tough competition and survive the battle. One's educational background is the most influential and powerful class divider that indicates one's family history and social status. Since the members of the whole household dedicate themselves to children's education which is viewed as the most important goal in life, their happiness and levels of satisfaction are ignored. In order to achieve such educational success, the entire family members collaborate together to sacrifice themselves for the best possible education for the children. In particular, the housewives are usually noted as the main person in charge responsible for their children's education. They will risk everything to place their children in the world's most prestigious universities. This, to a certain extent, explains why Koreans invest very heavily on private education regardless of family income.

Korea's educational fervor creates anxiety for all family members who are constantly struggling to keep up with and not fall behind the competition. The academic stress for children begins as early as when they are three to four years old, when they are in preschool. Consequently, most of the child psychiatric clinics are concentrated in the Gangnam area which includes the largest private education market in Korea. From a different perspective, the dedication and passion Korean people have for their children's education may be seen as the main hope and resource for a country that produces no natural resources. Is this really true? What or who is the education really for?

28 | Why do companies allow workers to come late on the day when the College Scholastic Ability Test is being held in high schools?

On College Scholastic Ability Test (Suneung) days, many people show up late to work. The airports nearby the examination centers prohibit airplanes from landing and taking off while nearby construction sites also suspend their work on the day of the examination in order to avoid distracting students with noise. All comprehensive preparations are made just before the examination day: the subway train schedule is adjusted, all the buses and taxies are mobilized, and even motorcycles are out in full force as an emergency transportation. Nothing can disturb any of more than thousand examination centers nationwide. To provide the best environment for the students taking the entrance examination, the nation and the people are fully mobilized, not to mention the students' parents, siblings, relatives, teachers, and juniors in the same school. Even the neighbors may have to be on the alert in case that the student's family needs their help on D-day.

The College Scholastic Ability Test is not just a test to prove students' academic ability but to determine their future that is very much dependent upon the university they attend. Since the friends and colleagues they meet in college influence their social authority and power, it is not an exaggeration in Korea to say that one's entire life depends on the result of the entrance examination. Thus, students study for hours on end, for their dear life. Their parents also pray diligently for their children's fate in churches and temples, as if they are sending their children to a battlefield. For those students who have studied day and night for 12 years to prepare for this particular examination, the test day means more than a regular holiday or even a national memorial day. I already mentioned the education fervor in Korea but consider the following 'modified' version of Charter of National Education to better understand the Korean education system:

> We matriculated into this school, charged with the historic mission of gaining an admission to a well renowned university. This is the time for us to prioritize our individual goals and contribute to the overthrow of friends without, by revitalizing the illustrious result of our seniors. We do hereby

state the proper path for all to follow, towards our preparation of college entrance examination. With the astute mind and feeble body, improving ourselves in the skills of college preparatory, ignoring the innate faculty of each of us, and overcoming the existing difficulties for our only standard of happiness, progress of grades, we will cultivate our cheating power and tact spirit.

After completing the ten-hour test, the long-suffered students are finally allowed to spend their time as they please. The very evening of the examination day is most bloody: some toast each other while others throw themselves in despair. All policemen are in a state of anxiety and tension preparing for possible aggressive behaviors. Everyone, including the students who have completed the examination as well as their parents, siblings, relatives, and neighbors, all feels the same way.

To cultural anthropologists, the examination day is one of the best opportunities to observe all types of religion in Korea. All possible talisman and charms are out on display. Traditional rice cake and taffy candies are the classic examples, and new symbols for wishing good luck emerge every year. Then after the test, the marketing wars targeting those who have just completed the examination begin. Such bizarre a scene of the examination day has been broadcasted worldwide several times but the picture of test day still remains unchanged. Would it be then more humane to take the test several times so that students can choose and submit the best score like in other countries? Rather, is it much more thrilling to stake everything on one and the only chance? Meanwhile, the examination day and all its wildness continue in Korea.

29 | Koreans work without taking any breaks. Why do Koreans live such a hectic life?

It is widely known that Koreans have the longest working hours in the world. In the past, Koreans worked hard to revitalize the economy that was devastated by the Korean War, but they continued to work hard even after the country joined the OECD. The government cut down the working hour to five days a week but Korea still has the longest working hours in OECD and the second longest in the world. Among 41 countries that the United Nations Statistics Division surveyed in 2004–2005, approximately 48.5% of the total population in Korea work more than 48 hours per week. Korea was only slightly behind the first ranked nation Peru where 50.9% of the total population worked about the same hours per week. Do Koreans really like to work? Or do they dislike taking a break? Why do they seem to have such a tough life?

Simply put, Korean people's life revolves around promotion in their workplace. When young people's entire life revolves around getting into a good college and after graduation, they continue to work hard to get promoted in their workplaces and to raise their salaries. A good college degree and a high salary are necessary for them to move from a semi-basement apartment to a better and more spacious apartment in a better district or region. Koreans always have a goal to accomplish and a dream to chase after, not just for themselves but also for their families. The economic development started since the 1960s and continued through the 1970s, 1980s, 1990s until now without ever stopping to take a break. Korean society keeps encouraging and persuading people to live for tomorrow and the day after tomorrow.

When did Korea achieve the 10-billion dollar exports and $10,000 individual annual income? Considering where Korea is today in terms of its economic power, it seems so long ago when Korea had one of the lowest GDPs in the world. Despite all that the nation accomplished in such a short period of time, people continue to desire for more developments and a better living standard. Such mentality demands that it is abnormal and unethical to take a break or not work hard enough. An anthropology textbook asks a question that Koreans would never have thought about: "Why can't Koreans be satisfied with working enough to get by and focus on quality of life instead?" This begs another question: Is the life of today's Korean workers who endure long working hours necessarily better than that of those living in under-developed countries?

The long working hours Koreans have do not always result in better efficiency or more productivity. Northern European states such as Norway or Finland are ranked first and second in national competence but their working hours are shorter than all other countries in the OECD. Such a simple fact confirms that taking a sufficient rest promotes better efficiency.

Of course, there are other factors that drive Koreans to work more than 50 hours per week. A few of the main reasons lie in individual expectation to earn extra income from overtime payment and the social expectation for the workers to sacrifice themselves for the company.

Once again, do Koreans really dislike taking a break so that they can work hard? No way. When they are off from work, they know how to enjoy themselves. They keep dreaming about breaking away from such a mundane and ordinary life when not at the office. They don't have time for introspection and reflection to think about how far they've come and where they are going. This might explain the reason why Korea's leisure industry is crippled. The real question I want to ask at this time is: "Are Koreans happy?"

30 | Why do Koreans like using seals more than signatures in legal documents?

Knowing that Koreans use seals is an interesting observation. But, do Koreans really prefer a seal over a signature? Of course, there are no statistics on how often a seal or a signature is used. But, there are really many cases of Koreans using seals, which might be striking to foreigners, who are used to signing papers. In addition to legally registered seals, there are also personal seals, which can be several and they are used according to different purposes. This practice can be seen as being illogical because seals can be lost and the possibility of people using fake seals is much higher than fake signatures.

A seal is an object, which is made of metal, wood or stone and is used to print any shape or name. But, the carving method, using method, shape and material of seals can be different according to the status of the person who uses it. For example, the seal used by a king was called a seal, *sae*, and nowadays the official seal of the Korean government is called country's seal or state seal, *guksae*.

Since when did Koreans begin to use seals? The earliest mention of it can be found in the myth of Dangun. This is the Korean foundation myth. The myth says that God's son, Hwanung, who came to human world, brought with him three different kinds of

objects to show his superiority and status. In the myth they were
called three pieces of In (印)[1]. *Memorabilia of the Three Kindoms*
(*Samguk Yusa*) says that these three things were a mirror, a sword
and a small bell, but nobody can say for sure whether they had the
same look or the same function of a seal. Even though, these three
objects originate from the myth and there is no real proof of their
existence, the oldest seal, which now exists, belongs to the Three
Kingdoms Era (57 BC -668).

Back in the past, Koreans did not use only seals. During the
Joseon dynasty (1392-1910), there was a practice called *sugyeol*,
which was not a seal but a kind of signature.

As the seal was a way of showing off prestige, commoners of
Joseon could not use seals, so they wrote their names in cursive
or semi-cursive letters. During that time, the high ranking
officials and other *yangban* (the upper class) also started using
handwriting instead of seals to approve documents. But for
illiterate people, even a simple mark was very hard to write.

There is one very interesting episode, connected with using
signatures in the past. When *yangbans* were buying or selling
land or slaves, they made a slave sign the legal document instead
of himself to sign. This signature was to draw a line around the
middle finger of the slave's left hand.

It might have been the influence of the Joseon dynasty, but, in
earlier modern times, a company's top executives and officials
tended to use signatures a lot. As a signature was considered a
privilege of the top class, lower ranking employees were kind of
restricted from signing and had to use a seal instead. Hence, cases
of using a signature or a seal slightly differ from each other.

Nevertheless, in the 21st century it seems to be a general
trend to use signatures. In the past writing one's own name was

a symbol of status and a way of showing off, but now there is no connection with signatures and status and everyone uses a signature.

V
TRANSPORTATION

31 | Why do people sitting in a bus or on the subway hold bags for those without seats?

How would people in New York or Tokyo react if you offer to hold their bags? They are likely to be very surprised and in the worst case, they might even think of you as a mentally-ill person. Why else would you suddenly touch and hold a stranger's belongings?

In Korea, however, many people often hold bags for those without seats. Nowadays, it is less common although just a couple of decades ago you could easily see people holding students' heavy bags. Most foreigners would not think it is bad to hold others' bags but they are likely to think such practice is strange.

Why would Koreans hold a stranger's bag? In the fundamentals of Korean society lies a very strong sense of community. Koreans often use an expression *sangbusangjo*, which means that life is worthwhile when people help each other. A long time ago, in Korea's past agrarian society, helping each other wasn't a choice but was required of a member of the community to share labor and care for others in common pursuit of happiness and harmony. Even when Koreans meet each other for the first time, they think of each other as relatives. A sense of family-like unity is strong in Korean society. There is a saying that even a single bean should be shared with others. There is always an exception and some people may not want to share a bean, but in most cases the social decorum expects people to put others' needs before oneself.

As Korea becomes more urbanized even these practices are changing. Everyone works for their own prosperity in a city and thus there is no need to share food and labor with others. Most people live in apartments and rarely get to befriend their neighbors. The city streets are crowded with people who are not related to one another. The main desire for them is not to be burdened or harmed by others, never mind helping and caring for the community.

32 | Why do people yield their seats to elders on a bus or train?

It might be surprising for foreigners to see Koreans standing up from their seats even when they are not getting off in order to yield their seats to the elders or pregnant women in a bus or subway. Even Japanese, who are known for their manners, are sometimes surprised to see such practice. We can easily find posts on the Internet when Japanese professors or workers living in Korea wrote about how they felt envious about it.

There were times when it was common to see elementary and intermediate school students remain standing even when there were empty seats. If an elderly person got on the bus, all young people and students stood up so there would be empty seats left. Times are changing and people don't give up their seats so willingly like they did before but they still do yield their seats. Now, special seats are reserved for elderly people and pregnant women. Young people, when they are tired, tend to close their eyes and pretend to sleep in order to keep their seats. Some old people don't even thank those who have given up their seats but scold them for having taken what belongs to them. It is thus quite understandable that less and less people are willing to yield their seats. Both the young and older generations are changing though not in a good way.

Despite the changes, today's Korean society still tries to maintain the seemingly logical and appropriate tradition of yielding seats for others. Since Koreans are very sensitive about age, doesn't it seem reasonable that young people give seats away and hope the favor will be returned to them when they themselves are old? They would become like those elders who haven't reached a high social status but still gain respect and protection for being old and especially for all their good deeds they did when they were young.

33 | Why are Korean bus drivers so aggressive? Why don't they follow the traffic rules?

When I get on a bus, I often recall a phrase that I have read somewhere before that Korea's traffic is so chaotic that it is even described in a children's song: "Ring, ring, ring, watch out! A bicycle is coming! Ring, ring, ring, you will get run over if you don't get out of the way." Listening to this song, Koreans would accept the fact that vehicles such as bicycles, buses, cars, and motorcycles have the first priority on the streets. I am not saying that there is no certain causal relationship between the song and the traffic problem. It seems undeniable that Korea's personal and material loss due to the badly regulated traffic system has the highest rate of accidents in OECD countries. It is no wonder that foreigners are fascinated by and fear Korea's traffic regulations.

Most noticeable is the bus drivers' reckless and wild driving skills that do not seem to be concerned with passengers or traffic regulations. Koreans seem very used to it and thus they get on and off the bus very quickly and with agility. When at the bus stop, you need to locate your bus and try to estimate exactly where it will stop in the long spacious stop area and move to the stop to get on it as quickly as possible. Actually, you should not "move" but race to the bus. The race continues on even if after you get on the bus. You should tag your transportation pass really quick and find a seat. If you have to stand on the bus, make sure to grab onto the handles very tightly and maintain your balance while the bus dashes through the traffic and car lanes and makes abrupt stops. Foreigners who have not experienced all of this, the whole process may seem like a great challenge. The bus drivers have gotten a lot better lately but their crazy driving is still problematic. Why are the bus drivers in such a hurry all the time? Herein lies some organizational and cultural aspects.

To begin with, the bus drivers have to drive as fast as possible to make the full round on a given time. The bus companies start each bus at every 4 to 5 minute intervals and complete as many roundtrips as possible in order to maximize their profit. There are disadvantages to the drivers who fail to follow the schedule and complete all the required rounds in a given time. The drivers then need to stay on pace with the bus ahead and keep the next bus behind them. In this process, a cut-in and indulging in signal violations becomes a must and not an option. And as a result, the drivers drive ever recklessly.

Buses in Korea are a major mode of transportation for most people and this fact is not likely to change for a while so passengers have no choice but to accept the bus drivers as they are no matter what. Compared to other advanced countries which have more convenient and safe bus operation systems, Korean buses seem dangerous and radical. Other countries' buses are an alternative means of transportation and run short courses whereas Korean buses are the most-widely used transportation method for millions of people who rely on the buses every single day.

Korean's admiration for "ppalli ppalli" or speediness is another indispensable factor which intensifies traffic problems. There are a number of passengers who urge drivers to hurry and drive faster so that they won't be late. They are pleased when their buses step on the accelerators and pass by the empty bus stops without stopping. Then they also criticize the drivers for violating the traffic regulations and driving recklessly.

Interestingly enough, Korean buses get weird compliments at times. When we travel abroad, we envy safe and accurate bus operation systems but on the other hand, some people get upset by such a system that makes the passengers wait forever for their bus and then to get to their destination. Another important merit about Korean buses is that they have a relatively cheap fare that by both young and old, rich and poor can afford.

34 | Why are there so many black cars in Korea?

Is it true that there are more black sedans in Korea than any other countries? There are quite a number of students who ask me why there are so many black sedans in Korea. This is a very interesting question but it is actually not an accurate observation. According to some statistics, approximately 35% of all cars in Korea are silver while 15% are white and 10% are blue and black, respectively. Red cars, a color favored by Italians, are very rare in Korea. Why then do foreigners think there are so many black cars in Korea?

Every country has black cars but Korea probably has the highest number of black sedans in the world. This also coincides with the fact that Korea has the least number of white, silver, or other bright colored full-sized cars equipped with over a 3.0 Liter engine. If you happen to come across a white-colored Hyundai Equus[1] on the street, then you are luckier than a person who has just found a four-leaf clover. In fact, I myself have never seen a white Hyundai Equus on the street in all my life in Korea. Then why is it that black cars are so popular in Korea, especially in mid- and full-sized segment?

The answer is quite simple; the color black represents authority and power. During the authoritarian period, the government was a symbol of power and its official vehicles were black. The preferred color choice was not only limited to the vehicles but also to other aspects of Korea. The robe, which represents legal authority in the court, is also black as are black clothes of the clergy that symbolizes sacred authority. To Korean people, even black sunglasses and gloves represents authority and power whether they are good or bad. Such symbols of power are further strengthened by the long line of black cars waiting for the members of congress at the national assembly building. Just imagine hundreds of black shiny cars lined up together. Their windows as well as those of the president's guard vehicles are all tinted in stark black that block any inside view. It is quite impressive that approximately 80% of 15 million cars that were on the streets of Korea in 2005 were sedans.

Unlike France which admires blue and Britain which admires green, Korea is full of very achromatic colors. In fact, Korean people could not freely choose the color of their own cars without

[1]
Equus was released in April 1999 and is currently being produced by Hyundai. It is a large size vehicle.

the permission by the government until 1986. The colors for the automobiles were first examined by the headquarters of the national police and then granted permission by the Ministry of Transportation. They were not allowed to choose either pure red or white because they were reserved for fire trucks and white police cars. These regulations disappeared while the government was preoccupied with preparation for the 1986 Asian Games.

Considering the speed of Korea's rapid development and transformation, two decades can be quite a long time. It would have been unimaginable to see so many different colors on the streets of Korea twenty years ago. And now, the automobile colors are becoming more varied with imported cars reaching 5% of all cars registered in Korea although most imported sedans still tend to be black. Black cars have somewhat of a proportional relationship to their prices because the number of black cars increases along with the price increase and vice versa. Such a pattern is unlikely to change at least in the near future.

VI

ENTERTAINMENT

35 | Why do Koreans enjoy going to a *noraebang* after drinking?

Koreans don't "always" go to the karaoke rooms after drinking, although the rooms have become a large part of Korea's night life. Karaoke rooms originate from Japan, but the number of karaoke rooms in Korea has overtaken Japan in the past decade and Korea now has the largest number of karaoke rooms in the entire world. Considering the thousands of karaoke bars and rooms nationwide, the annual revenue just from the karaoke business may be at least a few trillion-won. Why do Koreans like singing so much?

When people gather to drink, they often look for a karaoke room to take turns singing. It is very hard to imagine one not singing, and even foreign students hanging out with Korean friends end up joining at some point. Karaoke in Korea is more than simply a place where people sing. Many Koreans argue that they sing because they are either depressed or stressed out. Given that Koreans are not the only ones subjected to stress and that there are lots of other ways to relax, it is only more questionable as to why Korean people in particular like going to the karaoke rooms. In order to answer this question, we would have to look at the cultural background of Korea first.

Koreans are not especially talented singers or biologically proven to like karaoke rooms. Nowhere in the entire world would you be able to find listeners singing publicly on radio programs, sightseeing buses equipped with karaoke (although it is illegal now) machines, or TV programs such as *Challenging 1,000 Songs*[1] in which famous celebrities sing to karaoke music. Even on the streets, there is a constant sound of music whether it is from the

1
It is a famous TV program in which famous Korean celebrities sing randomly played songs from the Karaoke machine.

radio, television, or amplified speakers. These facts alone prove that there is more to it than Koreans simply loving music. When Korean people go to karaoke rooms, they go in groups as families, friends, or colleagues from work. It is also customary to sing along with each other rather than just sit in the corners and listen. Moreover, when selecting a song, one has to take the whole group into consideration instead of selecting songs that may destroy the friendly atmosphere. For newly employed workers, going to the karaoke room with fellow coworkers is a welcome ceremony they all must experience.

During the 1960s and the 1970s when Korea was undergoing a rapid modernization process, it seemed like a crime to enjoy leisure time instead of working. The famous slogan at the time was to "work hard and fight hard." Karaoke rooms became the sole and ultimate place for Korean people to enjoy their leisure time and show off talent they could not express elsewhere. People gathering together to enjoy each other's company while sharing food created the karaoke culture. To be more specific, the karaoke culture was created as a result of the historical experiences and social conditions of Korean people after the Korean War. Not everyone was able to adapt to such culture and sometimes suffered from terrible experiences of being forced to sing. Screaming and dancing to the music or singing along with others might prove to relieve stress but it may also expose the repulsive side of Korea's entertainment culture. Could there be other alternatives to karaoke rooms that are just as inexpensive and effective at relieving the stress of many people? By the way, there are also so called "luxury karaoke rooms" that target elites and those with high incomes. Korea is truly a karaoke paradise.

36 | Why do Korean films become so popular?

Considering the dominance of Hollywood films in the international film market, the popularity of Korean films is astonishing. How is it possible for Korean movies with a limited capital to often outsell Hollywood blockbusters in Korea? The domestic market share of Korean films is the greatest and in all the countries, only Korean films surpassed Hollywood films. Is it because the quality of Korean films is better than that of Hollywood? What makes Korean movies so popular? Before answering these questions, we need to first examine the following assertions. Some insist that Korean films are not necessarily more popular than Hollywood ones because Korean films take up a larger part of ticket sales than Hollywood films since people watch or download the latter from the internet. Korean films can also be accessed the same way but less so than the American films that are copied and purchased online. The same critics also add that the high-speed internet networks allow these downloading practices. Although we cannot prove such claims with accurate statistics, the illicit downloading cannot for surely explain the popularity of Korean films.

Others who do not agree with the aforementioned claim assert that the popularity of Korean films is based on the following reasons: First, some of the major companies invest in Korean film productions. These investments advanced the so-called Chungmuro film production system. Also, the 386 generations (people in their thirties, went to colleges in the 1980s, and were born in the 1960s after the Korean War) began to lead the film industry and brought about a groundbreaking shift in

Korean film history. In short, the implementation of a new film production system and the new generation of film producers allowed for the film industry to flourish. The film entitled *Shiri* is still remembered as the watershed moment in Korea's box office history and showed the Korean audiences that Korean films can be just as good as the imported ones. Secondly, the domestic distribution agencies and the distribution channels expanded throughout the country and so did the marketing strategies. The major companies also participated in these distribution and marketing processes. After the 1990s, the film industry took off and the maintenance of the screen-quarter policy[2] ensured that the domestic films have the most screen share in Korea.

The changing aesthetics of the audiences was another reason why domestic films dominated the box office. Thanks to rapid economic growth, Koreans are used to long working hours and as their income increased, they sought for a better lifestyle and leisure activities such as watching films at the movie theaters. Especially since many theaters changed into a multiplex that offers various shopping places, restaurants, and amenities, the moviegoers had more reasons to visit them with their families and friends. The screen share of Korean movies in addition to the major companies' financial investments resulted in a rapid development of the film industry. Of course, it has its own problems as well and some people are protesting to get rid of the screen share and completely open Korean markets to foreign films. However, the general consensus is that the growth of Korean film industry without screen quota system is still questionable. There are also others who criticize the shallowness of the mainstream Korean films that rely too much on comedy, action, and mob movies for purely commercial purposes.

2
It refers to the number of obligation days to screen the Korean movies in which it requires all theaters to show Korean films for 146 days or more in a year. This system has been implemented since 1966.

37 | Why are Korean soap operas mostly about family issues?

Compare the Korean TV programs with other countries and you will notice an interesting difference between them: Korea has the highest number of soap operas among other programs. On Korean public TV channels, excluding the cable broadcasting stations, more than 30 soap operas are aired on a weekly basis and most of these soap operas are about families. In other words, Korean TV programs are a paradise of family soap operas. Why do Koreans prefer family soap operas? There may be several explanations for this but of the main ones is the prevalence of so-called familism in Korean society.

Families are the basis of Korean people's life. They live for the family, by the family, of the family and such is the essence of Korean familism. The concept of family becomes a motivation for enduring any hardship and being a wonderful son or daughter is a final goal for many Koreans. Despite the dissolution and weakening of the family units, it is still strongly rooted in Korean culture which is built upon Confucian values. Singles or married couples without children are regarded as outcasts and immature even though they may be very successful in their professional and social life. For Koreans, forming a happy and harmonious family is an absolute task that demands self-sacrifice from all members.

The family relationship and structure might have changed from the Joseon dynasty but Korean people still value family as the most important basis of life. In this regard, the 'goose father'[3] that may seem strange to foreigners is regarded as a natural sacrifice one makes for the family. It is ironic that fathers need to part with their family for the sake of the family.

3
Goose fathers are the father who sent their young children to study abroad with their wife. They live alone in the country to earn money. Just like geese migration, they fly once or twice a year to a place where his family is living.

Korean viewers want a story closely related to their own real lives. What is remarkable is the wide variety of topics covered in the recent family soap operas. Most old soap operas usually focused on large families but recently, however, the family soap operas tend to deal with a more diverse aspect of family situations. Unlike the usual plot—a large family overcoming difficulties together—the recent soap operas show divorced families or second marriages. Such trend may also be a satire critiquing Korean families and challenging the concept of traditional familism. The unrealistic image of a happy family is criticized and thus the 'broken' or 'imperfect' family becomes central to Korean family soap operas. This is a very interesting and significant transition in Korean culture. The title of the movie *A Good Lawyer's Wife* (*Baramnan Gajok*)[4] and the soap opera *Spoiled Family* (*Bullyang Gajok*)[5] are some of the examples reflecting Korean families' move towards a new epoch.

38 | Why do Koreans like to go to a *jjimjilbang* just to lie on the floor?

Jjimjilbang which is translated as "hot sauna" does not fail to astonish first-time visitors of Korea. In fact, *jjimjilbang has* become a mandatory course for foreigners who want to experience Korean culture. The fact that *jjimjilbang* is spreading to places like America as well as Malaysia is something Koreans are very proud of.

Then what are Korean Hot Saunas like and why do Korean people go there to relax their back muscles? First, we have to understand Korea's *ondol* culture. For Koreans who have developed a peculiar

4

The movie A Good Lawyer's Wife directed by Im Sang Soo was first run in 2003. The original Korean title of the movie can be translated into Family of Having an Affair. Three members of the family including the married couple are having an affair. The couple brings up the adoptive son since they don't have child on their own. It depicts the figure of the family that is perceived as abnormal in the Korean society.

5

It is the TV drama aired in 2006. Through the story of abnormal family, it is a work that suggests the meaning of the true family.

heating system of heating the floors, lying on a warm floor is considered to be good for their health and is thought to be the basic but most essential aspect of comfortable lifestyle.

There is a continuous tradition of traditional healthcare methods in Korea. Some of them include saunas and public bathhouses where one would immerse themselves in the hot boiling water. *Jjimjilbang*, which in fact derives from the hot steams present in saunas, was invented from a traditional bathing culture. However, if we look at the current *jjimjilbangs* today, they are very innovative and modern. Such *jjimjilbangs* first emerged in the early 1990s and are still growing nationwide and worldwide. In short, the modern definition of *jjimjilbang* is not just a place where you take a bath but rather a complex area for various leisure activities. *Jjimjilbang* consists of lots of different theme rooms and activities and facilities such as a dining area, manicure and spa area, massage area, as well as swimming pools should rather be called a "*jjimjil* center." Moreover, it feels quite wrong to call a facility large enough to accommodate a few thousand people merely as *jjimjilbang* since *bang* in Korean means a room and rooms are usually designed for a few people. Consider the following advertisement:

> XX Korean Hot Sauna provides charcoal room, amethyst room, salt room, red clay sleeping room, forest therapy room, aerobic hall, sitz bath room, movie room, karaoke, PC room, amusement arcade, gym, salon, sports massage room, sleeping room for women, free yoga, diet, and aerobic lessons.

Most *jjimjilbangs* are open 24 hours a day and the entra-nce fee is usually six to seven dollars. During the early bird hours, you can use all facilities at a cheaper rate. *Jjimjilbang* is like a Disneyland for adults and is surely a place where people can take a bath, eat, play games or sports, and take a rest while hanging out with friends and family all at once for a reasonable price. *Jjimjilbang* has now become a part of modern Korean lifestyle.

Up close, *jjimjilbang* consists of a wide range of rooms, each representing the particular aspects of an ever changing Korean culture. For instance, rooms such as karaoke room and movie room were quickly incorporated into these large *jjimjilbang* complexes. Korean Saunas which were traditionally regarded as the leisure places where people gather together to relax on warm floor mats have now changed to what is called *jjimjilbang* consisting of the most modern and up-to-date facilities that the contemporary technology and popular trend can offer today. The already very popular *jjimjilbangs* are constantly evolving to differentiate themselves. Some *jjimjilbang*s even host special concerts to attract more customers. *Jjimjilbangs*, where hundreds of men and women get together dressed in the same uniforms and sometimes sleep together in a large hall, have now become one of the most vivid and amazing experiences for foreigners visiting Korea.

VII

KOREAN FOOD
& DINING

39 | Why do Koreans mix rice?

You may note the differences in culinary culture more quickly when you compare Koreans and Chinese eating *bibimbap*. While Koreans mix their rice topped with various ingredients, Chinese tend to separate the ingredients from the rice and eat them separately. In China, there is no such concept as 'mixing different ingredients' and rice being topped with ingredients is unacceptable. Considering many Korean dishes such as *bibim* Noodles and *patbingsu*, the 'mixing and eating' food culture has a long history in Korea. A Japanese cuisine that is served in Korea but does not actually exist in Japan is *hwedopbab*. Although a similar dish named '*sashimi donburi*' is served in Japan, it is still very different from *hwedopbab* which is basically a bowl of rice topped with raw fish slices and vegetables so that they are all mixed together with a hot pepper paste. Likewise, foreigners are often astonished by the color and shape of *bibimbap* that is topped with various kinds of seasoned vegetables.

The most widely recognized Jeonju *bibimbap*'s vivid color cannot be found in any other cuisine worldwide. However, it does not take long for our admiration of *bibimbap* to quickly change to a rather shocking astonishment. Why would one mix the beautifully topped and laid out ingredients? Some foreigners even express their concerns about mixing all of the ingredients together and thereby blurring or diminishing the taste of each ingredient. To a certain extent, this may be true but there is a distinct harmony of taste only found in the mixing of various ingredients. Then can it be said that such mixing of the ingredients does not lead to the 'destruction or ruination of taste' but rather to a 'creation of a new original taste?'

Bibimbap is a cuisine invented by a practical necessity. Although there are several disputes over its origin, the most persuasive explanation is that farmers in the old days invented *bibimbap* to eat more comfortably and quickly while working. Although others suggest that *bibimbap* originated at the royal court, both explanations underscore that *bibimbap* was created for convenience and efficiency. *Heotjesabap*, originating from Andong region, is also a famous variety of *bibimbap* that is basically mixed ingredients of various dishes served for *jesa*. Sharing food served to the ancestors during the rites with descendants and guests was simply more than just to fill one's stomach but was part of the ritual to consume sacrificial food and thereby sharing the good fortune rewarded by the worshipped ancestors.

Bibimbap which was once the common food during the periods of poverty is now becoming one of Korea's most representative traditional food dishes. Apart from its taste and practicality, *bibimbap* has another peculiarity: the act of mixing itself. Taking a big spoonful of the hot spicy paste called *gochujang* and mixing it with other ingredients and rice provides a sense of excitement that makes the people feel as if they themselves have fully completed the recipe. Finally, *bibimbap* is not only an individual's food source but it also evolved as a collective ritual behavior, most prominently as a large scale *bibimbap* feast in which thousands of portions of ingredients are prepared, put into a big bowl, and mixed together by all participants with a giant rice paddle. The finished product is then shared by all participants attending the event. Korean beliefs that "one needs to eat from the same rice bowl with others to become one family" combined with *bibimbap* ingredients has been called for such events and now serves as an important aspect of Korea's food culture.

40 | Why do people say that Koreans cannot live without *kimchi*?

Kimchi is Korean's unique fermented vegetable product for which cabbage, radishes, cucumbers and many other ingredients are preserved with salt and mixed with various seasonings including hot pepper, garlic, green onion, ginger, and salted fish. *Kimchi* is a side dish that is always presented on Korean dining tables and is considered to be the most basic food source in Korea that it is not even counted as a side dish.

The name '*kimchi*' is presumably derived from the term '*chimchae*' which means to soak vegetables in salt water. Gradually over time, the term '*chimchae*' underwent several alterations beginning from '*dimchae*' to '*jimchi*' and finally to '*kimchi*.' This process probably helps to explain why one of today's best-selling *kimchi* refrigerators is called '*dimchae*.' What did *kimchi* originally taste like? When looking back to *kimchi*'s entire food history, its red and spicy image is only a recent phenomenon. Various references from the three kingdoms period in Korea show that *kimchi* was simply radishes and cucumbers preserved in salt. It was not until the 18th century with the introduction of the pepper to Korea that *kimchi* which was spiced with red peppers became the staple image we know today. In addition, it was only after the Chinese cabbage (a.k.a brassica pekinesis) became largely popularized in Korea that *kimchi* was able to spread worldwide.

Although foreigners are astonished at the spiciness of *kimchi*, they are also surprised by the large variety of *kimchi* categories. The varieties of *kimchi* largely depend on the vegetables used as well as the regions of origins. Accordingly, one scholar suggests that the variety of *kimchi* outweighs the types of French cheese by a large margin. There are over 100 ingredients used to make *kimchi* and it is even harder to explain all the different recipes that apply different ingredients with different methods based on the region.

Although there are different ingredients and methods to making *kimchi*, it can be categorized into two main alternative forms: standard *kimchi* and *kimjang kimchi*. standard *kimchi* such as radish water *kimchi*, stuffed cucumber *kimchi*, and young radish *kimchi* is made to be consumed immediately and within a short period of time. It is also easier to make than *kimjang kimchi* which includes whole cabbage *kimchi*, *bossam kimchi*, and white *kimchi* that are preserved for a longer period of time for winter seasons.

Making *kimchi* has always been Korea's ancient custom and a big household event. The gathering of families in winter, where everyone participates in soaking the cabbages with salt and then mixing them with various seasonings, is recognized as a big festival rather than hard work. Given that vegetables can be obtained any time during the year in today's society, there is no more need to prepare an immense amount of *kimchi* for the winter season and has become a very tiresome practice. *Kimchi* is now mass-produced in food factories and sold in local supermarkets. Moreover, with the younger generations becoming more used to instant food, *kimchi* has now become a choice rather than a mandatory side dish and was nominated as one of the least favored food by elementary students. Children nowadays prefer pizza and hamburgers and one may wonder if *kimchi* will eventually disappear from the Korean dining tables in the future.

The quick answer is No. It is very unlikely that *kimchi* will ever disappear because it has now become more than just a type of food. According to some foreign journalists *kimchi* is the ultimate energy source for Korean soccer players just like how steaks are the source of energy for European soccer players. The mentality and strength of Korean people are often credited to *kimchi*'s spiciness and red chili peppers. From the viewpoint of food anthropologists, *kimchi* is not just a simple side dish but a symbolic food representing Korean's unique passion and value. Increasingly more and more foreigners who have become familiar with *kimchi* and its taste are again astounded by the nutritive value and healing powers of *kimchi*.

41 | Why do Koreans say they feel "*siwonhada*" (cool) when eating hot pepper broths?

Koreans feel 'cool' when eating hot and spicy food. They don't mean the temperature of food but rather, *siwonhada* (feeling 'cool' in Korean) refers to the feeling of being refreshed. Foreigners may find it strange when they see Koreans feeling cool and refreshed when eating hot spicy soup or enjoying spa at unbearably hot *jjimjilbang* (Korean dry sauna). A unique sense of Koreans— enjoying hot and spicy food to 'fight fire with fire' in the summer—actually helps to lower the body temperature in hot weather. When you sweat after having hot spicy food, you feel cool body temperature as your body dries sweat. When we drink cold beverages, they only cool down the esophagus and stomach momentarily but sweat from the body cools down the entire body.

Therefore, eating hot spicy food does help one to feel cool in a real sense. It is not easy for foreigners to eat hot boiling Korean broths full of red pepper or to enjoy a hot spa at *jjimjilbang* in the middle of hot summer. A considerable amount of time may be necessary for foreigners to empathize with the same kind of coolness and spit out the word, siwonhada! Even Korean children need some time to feel and enjoy this sort of coolness while soaking in the hot bathtub.

The distinctive eating habit of Koreans enjoying hot and spicy food triggers foreigners' curiosity. The image of *kimchi* with red pepper has now become a symbol of Korea's traditional food. Most tourists embark on the so-called 'kimchi adventure.' *kimchi* is not the only food drawing foreigners' curious attention. These foreigners may even experience a cultural shock upon seeing Koreans consuming raw peppers dipped in a hot spicy red-pepper paste. There is one difficulty that many international students studying in Korea usually experience. In order to avoid extremely spicy food, they usually check with a server before they order if it is spicy. Without any intention to deceive those students, most Koreans would say the food is not that spicy and worth trying. However, for those international students, the food on the table most often turns out to be not what they expected. Some international students would then ask in a different way, "Do you put hot peppers in it?" Koreans would reply, "Yes, a little bit, but it's worth a try!"

42 | Why do Koreans use spoons and chopsticks made out of metal?

Koreans didn't always use brass to make spoons and chopsticks. In the ancient times, chopsticks were made out of a variety of materials such as bronze, jade, and silver. The commoners utilized wooden chopsticks instead. There are several key rationales as to why brass spoons and chopsticks are still widely used today in Korea.

First of all, spoons made out of brass are much more resilient. It is an unquestionable fact that brass spoons can be used for a much longer period of time than wooden spoons. However, why do only Koreans utilize brass spoons but not other Asian countries like China and Japan that also use similar spoons and chopsticks? In order to understand this phenomenon, we need additional explanations other than its resilience. Currently, the Korean government is attempting to abolish disposable or wooden chopsticks used at most Korean restaurants. Provided the number of complications including the waste of resources and environmental pollutions caused by the disposable wooden chopsticks, their use was regulated by the government since the 1990s. This is the second reason which became the determining factor of settling on the use of brass spoons and chopsticks in Korean culture. Moreover, such regulations from the Korean government did not lead to the loss but rather benefits for restaurant owners and allowed for a more rapid settlement of the brass utensils in modern Korean society. Had we continued to utilize the light but insanitary wooden chopsticks, a considerable amount of resources would have been wasted and increased the expenses to dispose them. There is no doubt that such problems would have resulted in a national crisis.

Foreigners may find it difficult to even hold the chopsticks properly at first. Even Japanese visitors from a similar chopstick culture often need a while to get used to the heavy and slippery brass chopsticks. Being able to tear apart a piece of *kimchi* using only one hand and separate only one sesame leaf from the pile alone are captivating to watch. Lifting up a piece of soft jelly-like acorn pudding (*dotori mook*) without breaking it apart is no doubt Korean people's unique chopsticks skills.

Interestingly enough, there are different ways of using the same chopsticks and spoons in East Asian nations such as Korea, China, and Japan. Japanese people never use spoons when eating meals while Chinese people use them only for soups in which case a 'ladle' might be a more suitable term. Unlike in China and Japan, spoons in Korea are utilized as tools to eat rice and soup while chopsticks are generally used to pick side dishes. In short, chopsticks and spoons are more frequently used in Korea.

The length and the shape of the chopsticks also vary depending on each country's food culture. Out of the three countries, Chinese chopsticks are the longest in order to pick up food in the distance— in Chinese culture many people gather and enjoy their meal all together at a single table. Japanese chopsticks, on the other hand, are much shorter since Japanese dishes are served individually. Japanese chopsticks have very pointy tips to easily pick the flesh from the fish bones. The length and the tips of Korean chopsticks fall in between the Chinese and Japanese chopsticks.

43 | Why are *udon* and *japchae* served in Chinese restaurants? Why are pickled radish and onions served along with these dishes?

Before going any further, we should consider a few assumptions imbedded in these questions. Are we asking them the fact that *udon* is a Japanese cuisine and *japchae* is a Korean cuisine makes them unsuitable to be served at Chinese restaurants? Actually, both cuisines originated from China but were adopted by other cultures and modified and further developed to fit the local tastes. Both dishes no longer exist in China and are simply known today simply as Japanese and Korean dishes, respectively. Just like what Japanese people call *kimuchi* originated from Korean *kimchi* and modified for Japanese taste, *udon* originated from China's Tang dynasty. There are other views about the origin of *udon* but the most common and established theory asserts that a Buddihist Heungbub first took it to Japan after completing his study aboard in Tang. Likewise, *japchae*, which is known as a traditional Korean cuisine also originated from a Chinese dish made of cellophane noodles mixed with meat and vegetables. Of course, the modern version of such Chinese *japchae* uses thicker noodles with very different types of added ingredients.

Given what we now know about the origins of *udon* and *japchae* , asking why Japanese and Korean foods are served in Chinese restaurants may seem ironic. What is more interesting though is the way how *udon* and *japchae* came to be known as the signature dishes of Japan and Korea. There is another popular Korean noodle dish called, *jajangmyeon*, which is based on *jakjangmyeon* that originated from Shandong Province in

China many years ago. These two dishes of the same origin differ greatly in their taste. *Jajangmyeon* was first introduced to Korea in the 19th century and since then, it has undergone numerous alterations and modifications so that it would perfectly suit Korean people's taste and eventually gain a permanent status in Korean culture. Japanese *udon* follows a similar pattern in that it only shares a similar name with Chinese version of *udon* but they are very different from each other. It may be easier to think of *udon* and *japchae* served in Chinese restaurants as a few of the noodle dishes rather than those served in Japanese or Korean restaurants.

As for the pickled radish and slices of raw onions served along with these noodle dishes, anyone who has been to Chinese restaurants abroad will notice immediately that pickled radish and raw onions dipped in *chunjang* (black soybean paste) are only served in Korea. Although at times, *kimchi* is added to better suit Korean people's taste, the pickled radish and raw onions are the basic side dishes that are served in Chinese restaurants in Korea. With the increasing number of more luxurious and high-class Chinese restaurants, *jjachai (zha cai)*, seasoned peanuts, and pickled cucumbers are gradually replacing the pickled radish and slices of raw onions. In fact, the so called high-end and luxurious Chinese restaurants serving "authentic" traditional Chinese dishes are very much dependent upon whether or not they serve *kimchi* which is considered inappropriate and old-fashioned.

Anyhow, there are several interesting factors when considering the origins of both pickled radish and onion side dishes. Given that rice and sets of side dishes constitute a basic Korean-styled dining table, it seemed natural that Koreanized Chinese dish *jajangmyeon* also served with a set of side dishes. In general, the concept of side dishes doesn't exist in Chinese cuisines and it is only when *jajangmyeon* was introduced to Korea that the pickled radish and raw onion slices were served together. Similarly, those Italian restaurants in Korea also serve pickled vegetables as a side dish.

Then our next question should be to ask why pickled radish and sliced onions in particular are served in Chinese restaurants in Korea. The benefits of raw onion slices on greasy food are already well known but what is more interesting is that eating raw onion slices with greasy Chinese cuisines well suits Koreans' taste buds. It is also a well-known fact that radishes help digestion but the fact that picked radish allows refreshing one's appetite is more appealing to Koreans and has been acknowledged as one of the basic side dish for Chinese cuisines. If pickled radish and raw onion slices were not served in Chinese restaurants in Korea, perhaps *jajangmyeon* and *jjamppong* would not have lasted this long as one of the most popular Korean noodle dishes.

44 | Why do Koreans use toilet paper on the dining table?

It is natural for Koreans to see toilet rolls on the table. Many foreigners seem surprised and sometimes find them unpleasant, and Koreans in turn seem astonished by their reactions. For foreigners, the toilet paper has a very specific function that does not include being on dining tables. In reality, this kind of experience stems from cultural differences and may yield an unpleasant and serious culture shock to those who are not familiar with such differences. It would be a taboo for Koreans to use toilet paper on the table when in America so just imagine how Americans would feel when they see a toilet roll that belongs only in the bathroom located proudly on the dining tables in Korea.

Since when did Koreans start to use toilet papers on dining table? Better yet, when did they start using toilet papers? Before the invention of tissues, paper was a very rare resource in Korea so the history of tissue began only a few decades ago. Koreans know that toilet paper and tissues have a different usage but the former was introduced before the latter and were used for multiple purposes. Furthermore, toilet paper was cheaper and more convenient than tissues so it was natural for people to prefer them on dining tables. Now we can find a wide variety of tissues such as wet tissues, cosmetic tissues, and baby wipes but the toilet paper is by far the easiest and most convenient for everyday purposes. Kleenex in a paper box is fairly expensive so it has become a symbol for class disparities in Korea. A box of Kleenex instead of a toilet paper is often placed in the back seats of luxury sedans that are usually driven by company CEOs. Similarly, when Koreans invite someone important to their house, they remove the toilet paper and place a box of Kleenex or paper napkins on the dining table instead.

I once read a joke on the Internet about the ways to tell whether or not a foreigner has lived in Korea for a long time. One of them was when he or she becomes indifferent to the sight of toilet paper on the dining table. If foreigners do not feel unpleasant about it, then they have successfully adapted to Korean culture.

However, even the status of toilet paper is changing in Korea. Those who have lived abroad consciously avoid using toilet paper outside the bathroom because they are aware of the fluorescent whitening agents inside it. As more and more people become aware of these harmful ingredients in what they use to wipe their mouth with, toilet paper is gradually fading away from dining table. It is, however, likely that Koreans will continue to use toilet rolls as their favorite everyday supply if more environment-friendly toilet paper appears in the market.

45 | Why do Koreans cut beef with scissors?

The simplest answer: because it is convenient. Scissors can cut almost any food, including beef, noodles, and side dishes. However, not all convenient things are allowed in our society. For example, you cannot go around streets naked because it is cool and convenient. Likewise, using scissors to cut food can be weird in some cultures and sometimes frighten people from other countries.

Every country has its own culinary culture and rules. I have visited various countries and spent a fairly long time studying abroad but I still have trouble using certain silverware. Given the fact that Korean table manners are also quite complicated and strict, people could not have imagined using scissors in restaurants like nowadays. In fact, there is no accurate data to show us exactly when Koreans started using scissors to cut food. Judging from my experiences, though, it might have started around the late 1980s. In all possibility, using scissors started from the kitchen but gradually became a common practice primarily because of its convenience. The limited lunch time for workers forced restaurants to provide food as quickly as possible. Thriving

Korean style steakhouses decorated with water fountains and a small yard are often gigantic and bustling with customers grilling fresh beef on the table. And there, the waitresses always carry several pairs of scissors in their aprons. Impatient and quick-tempered customers who cannot wait for the waitresses rather take matters into their own hands and cut their meat with scissors themselves. People from countries that use knives and forks may not have thought about cutting their own steaks with scissors. No matter how convenient, they are not likely to change their "steak and knife" culture to "steak and scissors."

The same goes for Gal-bi. Gal-bi does not really go with knives and forks. Trying to decide which one is better at cutting meat is not a crucial matter. If you think about it, the food-cutting scissors are more related to modern Korean people and their lives. For them, it was important to quickly adapt to the rapid industrialization and modernization and somewhere along the line, the concept of 'faster and faster' became prevalent. As a result, things that could not have been imagined were created and experimented with in order to meet the changing needs of modern Korean people. In this sense, it might be easier to understand how and why Gal-bi met scissors on the dining tables.

46 | Why do Koreans put cherry tomatoes in desserts like cakes and ice flakes?

To begin with, tomatoes cannot be found in any of Korea's traditional food. In fact, cherry tomatoes were imported to Korea in the late 1920s and they were added to ice flake desserts and cakes in the late 1980s or foreigners who regard tomatoes as a vegetable find cherry tomatoes on top of cakes and ice flake desserts very exotic. This is almost similar to having a strawberry on top of rice; the two just don't go together. Then why is it that Korean people enjoy eating cakes and ice flakes desserts with cherry tomato toppings? The answer is quite simple. Korean people regard tomatoes as a fruit rather than a vegetable. Interestingly enough, tomatoes are in fact botanically proven as a fruit. If we define fruit as an edible substance wrapped around the seeds, then tomatoes would certainly count as a fruit. However, they can be horticulturally classified as a vegetable since they do not grow on trees but in soil. It only makes sense that Koreans add tomatoes to their desserts and cakes as both a vegetable and fruit. The whole notion that tomatoes are vegetables originate to countries that consumed tomatoes beforehand perceiving it as a vegetable served with the main dish. Nonetheless, Koreans classify tomatoes as an exotic fruit and thus to this day, tomatoes in Korea are sold in fruit stores.

47 | Why do Koreans hide dog soup in restaurants but state that dog soups are healthy?

The world first heard about Korean people's "love for dog meat" over twenty years ago. In the late 1990s, issues of dog meat in Korea became globally well known when a famous French actress requested Korea's president to take special measures to prevent dog meat consumption. Based on the written works of the foreign missionaries who resided in Joseon during the 19th century, we know that Korea's dog meat consumption was already known in other countries. This only became a serious international scandal since international events began to take place in Korea.

The dispute over dog meat became an issue during the 1988 Seoul Olympics especially among foreigners who believed such practice was uncivilized. Today's Mapo-ro Road was once called the Royal Road as many head chiefs, officers, and other VIP guests from abroad would arrive at Kimpo airport and pass by this road on their way to central Seoul. In due time, the walls would be repainted, old signs torn down, and although unseen today, the special fences disguised as signposts would camouflage the nearby poor hillside slums. The authoritarian government's main object was to hide the dark and ugly sides of Korea to the outside world.

Leaving a positive impression on foreigners would eventually lead to an increase in exports and improve the country's image and the dog meat scandal quickly became an obstacle to such national efforts. The scandal had more to do with the level of Korea's civilization than sanitary issues. The government's decision was very straightforward especially when the international media aired the whole process of Koreans catching and cooking edible dogs. The government requested that people consume dog meats in the back streets but not in public places. As a result, restaurants serving dog meat or broth moved to the back alleys and hid behind the signposts, *"yeong-yang-tang"* or nutrition broth and *"sa-cheol-tang"* or four-seasons broth instead. Not so long ago, however, the disputes over dog meat consumption became an issue again when the famous French actress previously mentioned protested against such practice. Those Koreans who supported the practice harshly criticized the actress as simply ignorant and rude. Korea's dog meat issue is often included in the various debates since both the opposing and supporting sides have very clear and valid reasons for their view points. Then there are others who believe that dog meat consumption is no longer necessary in the age of hyper or over nutrition.

So what's the end result of the dog meat dispute? Many restaurants serving dog meat still operate while the dog meat issue still remains controversial. Even some of Westerners consumed dog meat and treated it as an important nutrition since the agrarian society, it was an essential source of protein. Of course, dog meat is not the only source of protein and it is yet debatable whether or not dog meat contains more nutritious value than other types of meat. Considering Korean people's obsession with health and food, dog meat is likely to play hide and seek in the back streets of Korea for a long period of time.

VIII

RITUALS &
CULTURAL HERITAGE

48 | Why do Korean parents get so involved in choosing their children's marital partners?

Marriage practices and systems are some of the major fields in cultural anthropology. Marriage is a phenomenon that reflects matters about gender, blood ties, law in every society. Also, its culture varies depending on the region and thus standards of selecting a marriage partner are just as diverse. It ranges from where a spouse should come from, how many spouses an individual can have, who has the rights to select their own spouse: all these criteria are different in different cultures. There are not many places, however, where parents are indifferent and don't play any role in their children's marriage. The only thing that is different is their parents' influence and role in the whole process. In cultural anthropology, a common definition of marriage is found in Notes and Queries on Anthropology: "Marriage is a union between a man and a woman such that the children born to the woman are recognized as legitimate offspring of both parents."[1]

The image of romantic love that comes to mind nowadays is not really taken into account. In the history of civilizations, marriage was not a union of two individuals but a union between two families. It was a kind of exchange process based on partnership of two families a long time ago. In this context, it was not a matter of an individual selecting his or her spouse but rather a family duty.

In the patriarchal Joseon dynasty the person who decided on a proper spouse for their children was a grandfather or a father. Children's intentions were not really important so the bride and

1
Royal Anthropological Institute. 1951. Notes and Queries on Anthropology. London: Routledge. p.111.

the groom usually met each other for the first time at the wedding ceremony.

These days, a marriage with a spouse decided by one's parents is a very exceptional event. To be more exact, we should say that parents and children choose a spouse together. In modern Korean society, a good family background is still an important condition to become a preferable bride or groom. According to a recent poll, one's physical appearance and individual qualities as well as family background were chosen as some of the most important criteria for an ideal spouse. Basically, the traditional concept of marriage as a union of two families is still prevalent in Korea. That is why an intervention of the involved families is considered normal rather than the wishes of the couple in Korea.

The difference is that nowadays it seems unusual for someone to marry someone whom his or her parents choose but it also seems unusual for someone to marry someone whom his or her parents oppose. If children marry against their parents' will, they are likely not to receive any or much financial support from their parents and that could complicate their lives.

Nowadays, the process of selecting a spouse is a team effort of all family members involved. If parents don't have a wide range of social acquaintances that they seek for their children's marriage prospects, they use the help of some professional matchmaking agencies.

49 | When Koreans get married they sell *ham*, but what exactly is it?

After the families of the bridegroom and the bride agree upon a marriage, the former sends a letter to the latter to set the wedding date. After *napchae* the bridegroom sends wedding presents in a box called *ham* to the bride and her family. This process of delivering the presents is called *nappye*. The gifts usually include some jewelry as well as red and blue silk materials for the bride and her family. In the past, the bridegroom's male cousins or friends would carry *ham* to the bride's family who in turn would offer them a monetary gift or "*ham* compensation" to thank them for the delivery.

In addition to various gifts, such as silk materials and jewelries, *ham* includes a letter with the bridegroom's date and time of birth. It also contains another letter that officially acknowledges the marriage between the couple. In short, *ham* carries many significant and valuable presents that cannot be carried by just anybody. The bridegroom's family painstakingly chooses people with a good marital relationship and reputation to carry *ham* to the bride's house. They carry a traditional Korean lantern, called *cheongsachorong*, which has a red-and-blue silk shade signifying the bright future of the couple who will start a life together. Once the *ham* arrives at bride's house, the carrier put it on a top of rice-cake steamer. Chestnuts and jujubes are on the rice cake to wish the couple many healthy offspring. In the past, the formality of the wedding ceremony was a very complicated process and varied by the involved family's customs so the *ham* preparation was even more delicate and important event. These days, however, the wedding gifts are simply carried in a suitcase and most people do not really know the old traditional customs such as placing five different types of grain inside *ham*.

Some couples still prepare *ham* but with new customs and traditions. The carriers would still yell out, "Please come and buy our *ham*" as they walk through the apartment buildings to the bride's house in the evening. Sometimes, the male friends of the bridegroom become greedy over the *ham* price and annoy the bride's family. Neighbors who are usually very sensitive to the noise pollution understand that this is a very special day so they ignore the ruckus that the *ham* carriers are causing in the neighborhood. But the haggling over the *ham* price at times can get out of control and involve the police intervention. The bride's family has to welcome not only the bridegroom but also his male friends so they recruit young beautiful women who are still single to lure the *ham* carriers into the house to buy *ham*.

So how much is *ham* anyway? Unfortunately, there is no fixed price for *ham* but it cannot be too high or low so the negotiation process is very important. After selling it at a reasonable price to the bride's family, the *ham* carriers are served an extravagant dinner after which they go for a second round of drinks with the money they have earned by selling *ham*. The buying and selling of *ham* became a tiresome ordeal to the young generations so many bridegrooms deliver their own *ham* to the bride's family. This means that we now have a very slim chance of hearing, "Please come and buy our *ham*!" on the streets and the tradition of *ham* has become an old tradition we only hear or read about.

50 | Why is a Korean wedding ceremony so short?

There is no standard time duration for wedding ceremonies. Compared to Japan where wedding ceremonies and dinner receptions are held at the same place, Korean weddings are usually very short but definitely longer than the ones in Las Vegas.[2]

Traditional wedding ceremonies in Korea lasted several days or even several months. Christian or Buddhist weddings must be no longer than an hour lest the guests feel bored and uncomfortable.

Traditional Korean weddings consisted of several stages including *uihon, napchae, nappye, jinyoung,* and *pyebaek. Uihon* is an act of matchmaking, meaning a discussion between two families about the compatibility of the couple. After the bride's family sends a positive response to the proposal, the two families move on to the next step called *napchae. Napchae* is the process of setting the wedding date according to the bride and groom's *saju* or four pillars of destiny which predicts a person's destiny or fate. Once the date is set, the groom's family sends *nappye,* various presents such as blue and red silk as well as wedding clothes and official wedding document (*honseo*), to the bride's family. Then the two families finally celebrate *jinyoung* or wedding ceremony. Traditionally, it was held at the bride's house where the bride and the groom met each other for the first time. After the ceremony, the bride and groom traveled together to the groom's house. This procedure was very elaborate like a parade and was called *sinhaeng.* The bride then performed *pyebaek* to the groom's parents and relatives, also meeting them for the first time. *pyebaek* is a special bridal ritual of greeting the groom's parents and relatives by offering them a deep formal bow. When Koreans

2
See Kim Young Hoon(1996), The Commodification of a ritual process : an ethnography of the wedding industry in Las Vegas. University of Southern California: Social Anthropology.

get married, they often use expressions such as 'stepping into the bride's house' and 'going to the groom's house.'

Many of the traditional wedding customs except *pyebaek* are now replaced by Western-style wedding ceremonies that are altered to fit Korean culture. The most obvious alteration is the location of the ceremonies.

Usually, in the USA, the wedding ceremonies are held at churches, chapels, restaurants, or outdoors. In Korea, however, it takes place in a special wedding hall. Because the Korean population is highly concentrated in a limited land area, these wedding halls often get fully booked quickly on weekends. Approximately four or five couples get married in one place the same day so they are forced to end their ceremony as quickly as possible. Especially during wedding seasons, the wedding halls are so crowded that people say the staff members trail right behind the bride and groom walking out of the hall in the center aisle to roll up the carpet behind them. Sometimes the staff walks around the reception hall a few minutes after the banquet starts in order to rush the guests to quickly finish their meals.

51 | Why do Koreans change from a Western-style wedding dress into a traditional Korean dress during their wedding ceremonies?

When Koreans are asked this question, they would be a little surprised because they have never thought of it themselves. Do Koreans really change their outfits during their wedding ceremony? They actually do so for the *pyebaek* ceremony immediately following their Western-style ceremony.

Actually, changing clothes during wedding ceremonies can be found not only in Korea but also in other countries. A wedding ceremony itself is just a part of the wedding process but an engagement party or a banquet after the ceremony may be a part of the entire wedding process which requires different outfits. In Korea, after the Western-style ceremony is over, the bride and groom change into *hanbok* to perform *pyebaek,* which is part of the traditional wedding ceremony. In Japan, they also change clothes during the ceremony and banquet, which is called *oironaosi*, meaning a change of clothes three times. In Hong Kong, a bride usually wears a Western wedding dress during the ceremony but during the banquet with guests, she changes into a traditional wedding dress called *kwa*.

The Western-style wedding dresses were first introduced to Korea about a century ago. Since then, Western wedding dresses and ceremonies became a common practice but they didn't fully replace the traditional ones. Rather, they merged and formed a new style of wedding, consisting of both Western and traditional elements such as *pyebaek*. Such mixed wedding ceremony is one of the results of the various attempts to save Korea's wedding traditions. Most Koreans choose the mixed wedding ceremony although there are others who don't like the mixed wedding ceremony opting for a special wedding hall to hold a traditional ceremony instead.

In the past, the *pyebaek* ceremony was a ritual for the bride to greet the groom's parents and relatives. Traditionally, the wedding ceremony was held in the bride's house. The newlyweds then stayed at the bride's house for a couple of days and then moved to the groom's house. Upon arrival, the bride offered *pyebaek* food she brought from her house and gave a formal introduction in a form of traditional deep bow to the groom's parents and other relatives. The bride would first bow to the groom's parents and then from the closest to the farthest relatives. After that, relatives who have blood ties with the groom performed large bows to each other.

Finally, *pyebaek* food includes jujube fruits, chestnut, pine nut, and beef jerky all of which have different symbolic meaning. After the groom's parents receive bows from the bride and groom, they throw a handful of the jujube fruits and chestnuts on the bride's skirt to wish them many healthy children. A jujube fruit represents boys and chestnut girls. This tradition is still observed today but some newlyweds may not welcome too many chestnuts and jujube fruits since more and more Koreans prefer not to have more than one child due to the very high costs of bringing up and educating children in Korea.

52 | Why do Korean brides and grooms wear Western clothes and take wedding pictures in a royal palace?

When May comes, the royal palaces in Seoul get crowded with dressed up grooms, brides, and professional photographers. Watching all of them becomes unexpected entertainment for foreign tourists. What are these people doing? It is necessary to discuss several questions here.

The first question is about a change of clothes worn during the wedding ceremony, and second is from when and why wedding albums became one of the wedding traditions. Nowadays, Korean brides wear a white dress and veil, which is no different from Western countries. Grooms wear a tail tuxedo (maybe, first and last time in their life). Dressed like this, brides and grooms come to the royal palaces in Seoul, and take pictures there.

From when did Koreans start wearing Western wedding dresses? It started at the end of the 19th century, when Koreans started to accept new cultures and new styles, which meant to be Western. It wasn't easily accepted among Koreans, better to say, they were forced to accept it. For example, men were forced to cut the topknot of their hair, and those who refused to do it, were caught in the middle of the street and had it cut off. The modernization of Korea, when new culture was officially imported, dates back to 1894, when the Gabo Reform[3] was carried out.

The first record of Western wedding ceremony is closely connected with the spread of Christianity. Traditional wedding ceremonies, which were held in the yard in front of the bride's houses, moved to churches. Nevertheless, according to historical records, during the first Western-style wedding ceremony which was held in Jeongdong Church,[4] the bride and groom still wore traditional *hanbok*. As before, the bride wore a skirt, a jacket and rubber shoes, but only had a veil on her head. Starting like this, the number of Western wedding ceremonies increased; and, if we look at the pictures of weddings of 1930, brides already wore wedding dresses and veils similar to the West. The history of wedding dresses in Korea, which started 100 years ago, not only continues up to now, but the wedding dress industry has become more and more fashionable and developed. Koreans have

3
This is a reform movement promoted by King of Joseon, Gojong. Due to the movement, the conventional system of civilization including political, economic and social system was reformed into a new modern way.

4
It is the first Protestant church in Korea located in Jeongdong, Seoul. This red-brick chapel became a landmark of Jeongdong. The first pipe organ in Korea was installed in this church. The church was known as the Korea's 'high church' because of the location of the church as well as its Western design and high class devotees.

a tendency to choose very luxurious wedding dresses because of this lifetime event. Now, Korean wedding dresses are on the same level as those in Paris or Milan.

To capture this fancy and memorable moment, the bride and groom hire the services of the best photographers. In this new tradition, Deoksugung Palace has lost its original role and became a shooting studio. Deoksugung is the place where in the end of 19th century Emperor Gojong[5] lived and died. But nowadays Koreans seem to be indifferent to their country's past. They cut their hair on their own will, wear Western clothes, pose and take pictures in front of Gojong's office.

Outside photography shoots became an unchangeable tradition of Korean weddings since the 1990s. The bride and groom take pictures against the background of palaces or gardens in order to compose several wedding albums. Depending on the studio, level, size and number of pictures, these albums can cost from hundreds to thousands of dollars. If the video recording is also used, the price can be very astonishing. Just 40 or 50 years before, taking a taxi after the wedding ceremony and having a ride around the city was considered a luxury.

5
The 26th King of Joseon dynasty (1852-1919)

53 | When Koreans marry they say they will serve the noodle for the guests, but in fact, it is hard to find noodles in the wedding. Why does this happen?

The simple answer is that noodles are no longer the main menu at weddings ceremonies nowadays. If noodles were served as the main menu at the wedding receptions, the guests will never cease to stop talking about the hosts behind their back. The common consensus is that the hosts should at least serve *galbitang* (short ribs soup) or buffet of various kinds.

There are several reasons why Koreans serve noodles at traditional parties and wedding receptions. Noodles used to be one of Korea's special dishes and signified health and longevity. Noodles are also easy to digest and to serve so they were most suitable dish to be served at the wedding receptions. That way the guests could pray for a long and happy life for the newlyweds while eating. Koreans still remember such tradition and instead of pestering unmarried singles about marriage, they simply ask, "When are you going to serve me noodles?" Just like other old traditions, noodles are also disappearing at parties and receptions these days. They are merely served at the wedding banquets to provide an assortment for the main menu. Will they completely disappear someday? I wonder if what they stand for— the longevity—would prolong or sustain its life in contemporary Korean culture.

54 | Why do Koreans put food, alcohol and even cigarettes on their ancestors' tombs and why do they perform a big bow, called *jeol*,[6] in front of the tomb?

6

Jeol is to greet and show respect to others. There are different types of jeol depending on the subject or situation. Koreans perform keunjeol to greet and show full respect in ceremonies like ancestral rituals and weddings.

Koreans have a unique way to show respect for their ancestors that is different from memorial ceremonies in other countries. Koreans prepare special foods and they perform *jeol*, a large bow in front of their ancestor's tomb. These rituals are done as a sign of respect just like many other cultures have special rituals to show respect in their own ways. But a lit cigarette placed in front of a tomb and bowing can be a strange thing to see if one is unfamiliar with Korean culture. Does the owner of the tomb really still smoke? To understand this memorial ceremony, it is necessary to understand Koreans' attitude towards their family members who have passed on.

In Korean culture, respect for ancestors is of great importance. Koreans pray to their ancestors twice a year, at Chuseok (Korean Thanksgiving Day) and at Seollal (Korean New Year). Both holidays follow the lunar calendar and the main purpose is to show respect for the dead. During this time the highways throughout Korea become congested with traffic. A trip across the country usually takes about five hours but during the holiday, the travel time can well exceed 10 hours. But why do the roads become so crowded? People are returning to their hometowns to pay respect to their ancestors. They prepare a special worshiping ceremony called *jesa*.

Jesa has a long history beginning during the Joseon dynasty when the country followed Confucian philosophy. Confucian ideology believes that filial piety is the most important platform of a strong and peaceful society. Back then, people showed great respect for their parents and those who came before them. Not only is respect for one's parents important but it also connects new generations to those generations gone past. People get to know their family history through the ancestral ceremonies they performed. At that time, people did not travel much throughout the country. Families stayed within one region and ancestors were buried there. These family areas became significant in that they represented generations and generations of one family's history. Today the meaning has been carried forward. Confucianism remains rooted in the culture and people still return to the place where their ancestors lived to perform *jesa*.

The symbolism of *jesa* is very simple. The action of *jesa* shows that those living still remember those dead. During *jesa* people remember their ancestors as though they are still alive today. Koreans greet their elders with a small bow in the morning and evening. In *jesa*, a big bow is like a greeting to the dead. People also prepare their ancestors' favorite foods to offer to them. In the ceremony the ancestors come to the table to eat the offering. In Western society people place flowers in front of the tomb, while in Korea people prepare food and alcohol for the dead. These actions carry similar meaning. If a person enjoyed smoking when he was alive, even after his death, the family can place a lit cigarette in front of his tomb so he may continue to enjoy his pastime.

The ritual of *jesa* can be very strict. The preparation of the food and its arrangement is very complicated and depends on the general rules of the ceremony. According to the region and times, the ceremonial rules can be different but there is always a specific procedure to follow. *jesa*, performed at home, and *jesa*, performed in front of a tomb, can be different, too, but the basic meaning is the same.

Jinseol are the rules for arranging the food dishes and includes *eodongyukseo* (fish east, meat west) or *hongdongbaekseo* (red [fruit] east, white [fruit] west). Fish has to be placed in the east while meat should be in the west. As well, the tale of the fish should point east and the head west. In regards to the placement of fruit, red fruits—usually apples—should be placed on the east side of the table while white fruit—commonly Asian pear—should be placed on the opposite, west side of the table. These examples are a few among many rules governing the preparation of the food used for the ritual. Of course, there is no rule about cigarettes. These days the favorite foods of the dead are changing, so people place cigarettes, chocolate pies, pizza or anything else that person might have enjoyed on the ceremonial table.

55 | What is special about Korean funeral culture?

A lot of Japanese people talk about some interesting findings after they experience the funeral culture in Korea. First of all, there is no monk in Korean funerals. When a family holds a funeral, they generally serve their guests with Korean soup called *yukgaejang* which is a hot spicy meat stew. Some guests spend hours playing the Korean card game *hwatu*. Japanese people are curious about the fact that Korean people hold a funeral at the hospital where one died. In a nutshell, the spirit of the deceased cannot return home. Compared to the wedding ceremonies in Korea, some say that Korean funerals still maintain more traditional elements even though they have changed a lot over the years.

Let's now take a closer look at the process of the traditional funeral in Korea. An old man on the verge of death is carried to the main room of his house and all of his family members and friends share his last moment. This process is called *imjong* or deathbed. If a person dies when he is away from home, people used to consider his death to be tragic. An ideal death in traditional Korea would be to die in one's own main room. As previously mentioned, the best time of one's death is when his or her children and other family members are present. When a son or a daughter misses the last moment of his or her parent's death, it was considered to be the most unfilial act.

The traditional funeral process takes three days. When someone passes away, one of the family members goes out to the yard or up to the rooftop to wave the dead person's clothes and shout "bok"—meaning "come back again." They all know that the deceased will never come back but they still call out to the dead in sorrow. Then, the family members put up a screen in front of the dead and they dress up as the mourners and inform the others about the passing of the deceased. On the second day, the deceased is washed and then clothed in a new funeral outfit. They also put three spoons of rice and a coin inside the mouth of the dead so he or she will have enough food and money for the final journey to the afterlife. The corpse is put on many layers of shroud and tied from head to toe. After this process, the corpse is placed inside the coffin and finally the funeral is held on the third day.

A good burial site is selected by *feng shui* or geomantic principles. After the three year mourning period, the funeral process is officially over. Of course, the offsprings of the dead continue to hold a memorial services on the anniversary of the deceased every year. However, it is hard to find people who observe a three-year mourning period these days. There are some families who still hold a memorial service strictly in Confucian tradition but it is very rare that such families make headline news for their endeavors to observe the tradition and become a valuable source for some documentary writers. Park Chul-soo's film *Farewell My Darling* (1996) was highly praised for its illustration of Korea's traditional funeral rites.

As I mentioned earlier, Koreans now die in hospitals. In the old days, there were not enough medical services so it was natural to breathe one's last breath at home. Most people who suffer from a terminal illness face their death in the hospital room nowadays. It seems practical especially since those who live in the city would not be able to provide enough space at home to accommodate all the funeral guests. Because it is convenient and efficient, most people use the hospital funeral parlor which offers round-the-clock service. There is no need to worry about complicated funeral arrangements or food preparations. Despite many changes in the funeral process, most Koreans still keep the three-day mourning period and bury the dead on the third day after the death. That being said, those with a special position or status are an exception.

After finishing the funeral ceremony on the third day, all family members take the coffin to the burial plot by a funeral coach. The female family members wear a white mourning dress, but the male members wear black suits with a black tie rather than the traditional mourning dress. Instead, they wear a traditional linen armband over their Western-style black suits as a way to assimilate tradition to modern lifestyle. Three days after they bury the dead, the family members revisit the burial site to hold memorial ceremony and after the first year memorial ceremony is held usually at home every year.

All in all, the funeral process may have been simplified but it is still common for the family members to avoid too many accessories and behave very discreetly. To show the period of mourning, men wear a white ribbon on their breast pocket and women wear a hairpin with a black ribbon in their hair. Close friends or acquaintances also need to respect this period and be discreet around them. Along with many changes in this fast-paced and complicated modern society, Korean funerals have become a lot faster and easier compared to the past.

56 | What is *ondol*?

The most distinctive characteristic of Korea's traditional house is the wooden floor heating system. The system combines two different residential types, each suitable for all seasons especially cold winter and hot summer. While the heating system originated in the cold northern region, the wooden floor originated in the hot southern region for the purpose of cool air ventilation. The two systems were finally combined during the Goryeo dynasty. Accordingly, the floor heating system is often regarded as one of the more fascinating Korean inventions with its peculiar and distinctive heating method. Although China's northeastern region has a floor heating system of its own, it is only used in sleeping quarters whereas Korea's heating system heats up the floor of the entire house.

The way the floor is heated is fairly simple. First, add wood and fire in the furnace so that the heat warms up the floor, which is made out of flat stones. In more technical terms, it is a radiant heating system where the heat from the furnace is transmitted to the flat stones which in turn heat up the floor on them and eventually warm the entire house. Such a simple floor heating system is regarded as an outstanding heating system because of its efficiency and practicality, which also allow cooking and heating to be performed simultaneously through the same source of heat. Moreover, it is a very reliable and resilient system that can be used for many years.

The floor heating system, however, has its own limitations: an extensive heating time and the difficulty of controlling the temperature. Despite such problems, the floor heating system provides more than simple warmth to Koreans. It is a part of Korean tradition that led to the Gudeul Culture, which became a basis of Korean ideas such as: "Be born on the heated wooden floor, die on the heated wooden floor, and eat food for ancestral worship service on the heated wooden floor." The Gudeul Culture also gave rise to other unique clothes and food customs that have become deeply imbedded in the Korean way of life. Although the traditional heated wooden floor has mostly disappeared today, the concept has been applied to modern apartments which use the same method but rely on oil instead of firewood to heat the floors. And instead of a furnace, pipes or coils are built underneath the floor to heat it up. This modern method is also known to be very energy efficient. Moreover, the practice of taking off shoes after entering the apartment and before stepping into the apartment floor is also very much related to the traditional heating system culture and rarely seen in Western culture. As previously mentioned, traditional Korean houses have been replaced by apartment buildings and complexes and other Western-style houses but the *ondol* culture are still preserved to date and have evolved into other distinctive cultures of their own.

57 | Why is Hangeul highly praised around the world?

The greatest achievement of mankind's history is speaking languages and creating alphabets. Such abilities have built the foundation of today's civilizations. Linguists say there are numerous words and languages around the world, created, changed and disappearing over time. The number of perished alphabet reaches as many as 900 so far. It is believed that the Sumerians invented the first writing system, a wedge-shaped character inscribed on clay tablets. Old Chinese, the language with the largest number of speakers, was invented 5,000–6,000 years ago. Compared to this, the native alphabet of the Korean language Hangeul has a relatively short history: It was created in 1443 and its script was promulgated in 1446. Hangeul's official name is Hunminjeongeum, literally the "right words that teach the public." Foreign scholars also recognize the excellence of Hangeul. For example, an American linguist still celebrates Hangeul Day (October 9) to honor the invention of Hangeul. Interestingly, Hangeul proved its excellence thanks to cellphone texting. Hangeul is the fastest and most efficient alphabet to type message compared to Chinese, Japanese and English. Koreans on the subway sending text messages with their cell phones intrigue foreign visitors. For foreign scholars, it is easy to explain what makes Hangeul an excellent writing system, not easy to explain for Koreans.

First, Hangeul is a systematic and ingenious writing system. It takes the shape of the articulation organs including the tongue or lip as they form sounds. Hangeul is a very simple but very systemic alphabet in creating derivatives. For example, the consonant ㄱ is changed into ㅋ and ㄲ.

The vowels are based on three universal principles, including the sky (•), earth (—), and person (|); these three factors are used alone as well as in combination. Second, 24 consonants and vowels are distinguished simply by shape. In addition, it is possible to write more than 11,000 Hangeul characters. Third, Hangeul has an inventor and specific date of creation. Most languages in the world have evolved to what they are now, with no records regarding their inventors. However, Hangeul and its features are described in the *Sejong Sillok*, an official record of the king's affairs. Fourth, the UNESCO created the 'King Sejong Prize' in 1989. The prize is awarded to individuals and groups who are recognized for their contributions to curb illiteracy. In 1977, *Hunminjeongeum* was registered as Memory of the World in recognition of its historical value by UNESCO. Of note, Hangeul's convenient and efficient features are helpful for those with no writing system.

58 | What is *samullori*?

Samullori is a Korean traditional quartet with four instruments; *kwaengwari, jing, janggu* and *buk*. Created in February 1978, it has a short history and is also referred to as a new kind of art having an impact on the public. Sharp and ear-splitting sounds of *samullori* fascinate the audience. Controversy surrounds whether it is traditional folk art or not. The sounds generated by the four players bring the audience together. This is called *shinmyeong* (cheerful and spirited feeling in Korean). *Samullori* has its roots in Namsadangnori (one of Important Intangible Cultural Properties) or wandering artist-entertainers. They wandered around but boasted outstanding performances and an artistic spirit. This is because they were trained under strict conditions, believing their dedication to Korean music is the source of living. For years, what is traditional has been viewed as old-fashioned, pseudo-scientific and something to break away.

However, in the early 1970s, the campaign to revive *talchum* (Korean mask dance) left a profound mark in the nation's traditional art history. The move gained popularity and became widespread nationwide. In line with the move, the traditional art preserved in local areas were actively explored and handed down. As a result, the Korean shamanic ritual *gut*, which had been overlooked, received academic focus. Korean traditional percussion music also received attention. The percussion band grew to be embraced by office workers, housewives and so on. It further expanded to reach social education groups and labor circles. *Samullori* propelled a surging interest in the *pungmul gut* ritual, which had been in the spotlight. NANTA, a popular show inspired by traditional rhythm and *samullori*, has gained millions of global viewers and gives dynamic and energetic images.

IX

BELIEFS & VALUES

59 | Why is the Chinese zodiac important to Koreans?

The Chinese zodiac is a system where each year is symbolized by an animal, according to a 12-year cycle. Koreans follow this Zodiac system, and when a person is born, he/she automatically receives a sign. The sign depends on the year the person is born. For example, if the person is born in the year of the Pig, he has the Chinese zodiac sign of the Pig.

Why is each sign related to an animal? From ancient times, people lived close to animals. In agrarian societies, in particular, the labor of animals was closely connected with people's survival. Because of this important role, animals became sacred symbols. For example, a cow or ox was a key element in farming. It became a symbol of faithfulness and virtuousness in work, and became a worthy example for people to follow. A tiger had courage and power and became the symbol of respect and fear and was placed almost on the same position of a mountain god. The tiger is one of the most important symbols in Korean culture. If you visit famous mountains and Buddhist temples in Korea, there is always a separate shrine for the mountain god and the tiger is painted together with him. Especially, the combination of a human's body and a tiger's head is often portrayed in such important places as the main hall of Gyeongbokgung Palace as one of the major patron saints of Twelve Earthly Branches. Twelve Earthly Branches is a Chinese ancient system of reckoning time, based on observations of Jupiter. The orbit of Jupiter was rounded to 12 years. The twelve years of the Jupiter cycle also identifies the twelve months, twelve animals, directions, seasons and Chinese zodiac hour system.

Symbolic animals play a very important role in Korean culture and are closely connected with notions of time, space, and direction. In the Chinese zodiac, there are twelve animals. Starting from the Rat, the order is Ox, Tiger, Rabbit, Dragon, Snake, Horse, Goat, Monkey, Rooster, Dog and Pig. Koreans usually refer to this order in Chinese characters: Ja (子), Chuk (丑), In (寅), Myo (卯), Jin (辰), Sa (巳), Oh (午), Mi (未), Sin (申), Yu (酉), Sul (戌), Hae (亥).

What were the criteria in selecting these animals and placing them in this order? These twelve animals are identified by a 12-year cycle, as mentioned above. But it is also believed that it comes from the astrological calendar of Islamic civilization. The principle of placing animals in this order is derived from the Chinese hour system, based on double hours. It is said that in the first period from 11 pm to 1 am, a rat is the most active animal, then from 1 am to 3 am, ox eat grass, getting ready to plow. Like this, each next double hour period is connected with an animal, according to its attributes. The last period from 9 to 11 pm is a pig because it sleeps the deepest during this time.

This principle of relating animals with time and year also has a functional meaning. Koreans believe that the fortune of the year and person's inborn character are closely connected with animals' attributes and looks. For example, it has been traditionally believed that the year of the Dragon is peaceful. The one who was born in the year of the monkey has a lot of skill and person who was born in the year of the tiger is very brave. These beliefs are connected with traditional philosophy of The Five Elements[1] and can be used as a tool to predict destiny and even the flow of social change.

For modern Koreans, the Chinese zodiac is generally a system that helps to learn about personal character and relationships with

1
The concept of Five Elements is from the philosophy of ancient Chinese in which the universe is made up of the five elements, which include gold, water, tree, fire and soil.

other people.

Nowadays, the beliefs of the Chinese zodiac and its influence on destiny and character can be found in three fields. The first one is making a prediction for the year according to the year's animal. For example, the year of the horse is supposed to be filled with energy and vitality, according to a horse's properties. As it was mentioned before, the Chinese zodiac animal is closely connected with a person's character. The last one is the comparison of Chinese zodiac signs of two people before marriage to find out their marital compatibility. This marital compatibility (*gunghap*) is a very interesting concept which stands for a harmonious combination of energy of two people beyond just physical compatibility. The prediction of marital compatibility is the best known area of using Chinese zodiac system in Korea. This compatibility is decided by how well two animals match with each other. For example, both a quickly moving mouse and a monkey is a good match for each other, but a field-working cow doesn't really suit a working horse.

But this job of predicting destiny or relationship between a groom and bride requires special practice and personal abilities. In Korea, special services of fortune telling using Chinese zodiac is widely spread. Plenty of advertisements in newspapers and on the subway show that fortune telling is exercised as a kind of industry. Do Koreans really believe that their Chinese zodiac sign determines their future and destiny? It seems this traditional belief has transformed in entertainment.

60 | Why do Koreans prefer to marry a man who is four years older than a woman?

According to the Korea National Statistics Office (KNSO), there are more than 10 million couples in which 80% of them are comprised of couples whose husbands are on the average 4.2 years older than their wives. Such information allows us to statistically prove and validate the above question. Why is the age gap specifically four years? Before we explore this question, we need to first investigate the assumption that husbands should be older than wives in marriage.

During the Joseon dynasty, people married at a much earlier age and it was common to see an older woman married to someone much younger. Considering that people had a much shorter life expectancy at the time, it is understandable why people got married at a very early age but the reason as to why women were older is yet uncertain. Though there are no precise statistics to perform an analysis on the age of married couples in the Joseon dynasty, it is an inevitable fact that the optimal age for marriage has changed and still is constantly changing over generations and for various reasons.

Although today's married couples seem to set their own rules in keeping a four-year age difference, it is still difficult to explain why married couples consists of a diverse range of age groups. For instance, married couples in their 60's have a different background and meaning to their marriage age or the age gap when compared with recently married couples.

A man-woman relationship and the roles of husbands and wives differ from one culture to another but in general, men tend to have a more superior position within the family and are in charge of the whole household. However, it should be noted that the stereotyping of a husband as an older brother and a wife as a younger sister is quite a recent phenomenon. Looking back at the entire human history, anthropologists state that it has been only in recent years that such notion emerged to the surface.

Other than the basic condition that a husband should be older than his wife, the specific preference for a four-year age difference may be explained through Korea's fate and marriage compatibility test that is based on the belief that a person's fate is determined by his or her date of birth. To be more specific, one's fate is decided by the year, month, day, and hour of his or her birth. Accordingly, the marriage compatibility tests how well one may get along with his or her marital candidate based on the fate that the potential partner was born with.

People born in Korea are assigned to a specific Chinese zodiac sign depending on their birth year. Beginning from a mouse to a pig, there are 12 different animals constantly rotating and the animal assigned to the year of one's birth becomes the individual's particular Chinese zodiac sign. The 12 different animals share different relationships with each other. For instance, rabbits and monkeys do not get along with each other whereas horses and dogs are quite a good match. In other words, those born in the year of rabbits are likely to have an uneasy relationship with those born in the year of monkeys and likewise, those born in the year of horses will maintain a good relationship with those born in the year of dogs. The animals that maintain a balanced and harmonious relationship with each other have a four-year age difference, thus suggesting that such age gap between couples would yield a good marital relationship.

It seems strange that the fate of all individuals can be determined solely by one's Chinese zodiac sign not to mention the relationship each animal has with each other. Calculating one's fate and marital compatibility is still commonly practiced by parents of both families before marriage so much so that the custom itself constitutes an independent service industry. Nowadays, the number of couples in which the wife is older than the husband is gradually increasing, implying that conditions other than marriage compatibility and age differences have become more important. The ultimate question is can "love" be free from fate and marital compatibility.

61 | Why are Koreans reluctant to write their names in red?

Every culture has taboos, rules and regulations, which reflect customs and cultural protocols. There are various kinds of taboos on colors, and each color contains different meanings in different cultures. The same color can have opposite connotations in different contexts. Some might consider those taboos as marginal aspects of a culture but their powerful influence may be felt when they are broken.

Koreans do not write their names in red because doing so represents death. The names of the dead are written on the cover of a coffin in red. Koreans draw a red line on the name of the dead in family registries. It is said that the name of condemned criminal is also written in red ink upon sentencing. Writing one's name in red, therefore, becomes a curse and death.

The color red has a wide variety of meanings: from death

to birth. While it is just a single color, the meaning of it forms a spectrum. Eating red bean porridge (*pat-juk*) on the winter solstice, or hanging red pepper on a straw rope are some of the customs originating from the belief that the color red has a power to exorcise evil spirits.

Then, why have Koreans come to consider the red color as a symbolic and sacred color among all the others? One of the most primitive experiences that human beings have may be the sight of the Sun, the source of all lights so the color red represents the Sun that also symbolizes the source of life. This mighty color has a sacred power and is used to exorcise darkness and demons. People build red gates with spiked top, write an amulet and talisman in red, and the shamans shun red roses because the evil spirits and ghosts are afraid of the color. The spectrum of red does not cease here. After the South Korea-Japan World cup in 2002, the Red Devils[2] became the most significant symbol for Korean soccer.

The fervent cheering squad, Red Devils got its name because they were all dressed in red. The Reds surely gave foreigners a strong impression. So why the Red Devils? The roses given to one's sweetheart mean not just flowers but also one's dedicated and passionate love. There was once a foreign media outlet that assumed the success of Korean soccer lies in *kimchi* consumed by Korean soccer players and many other foreigners associate *kimchi* with hot red peppers. From red devils to red pepper, the color eventually became a symbol for Koreans' passionate nature. Koreans, once known to dress in white, now favors for being colored in bright red colors.[3]

The color also reminds Koreans of another taboo. With extreme antagonism between South and North Korea, the red symbolized the North, totalitarianism. Calling someone a *"bbal-gaeng-i,"*

2
It is a supporting organization that was formed voluntarily by Korean soccer fans in December 1995 in order to support the national soccer team of South Korea.

3
The country was once called 'the ethnic group of white coat' in the sense that Koreans dressed in white for a long time.

meaning the "red commies" in English, was the most terrifying curse one could say to another in South Korea. Many so-called "*bbal-gaeng-i*" are executed and the color red became a sinister sign thereafter.

Soon, the world changed and so did the meaning of red. Now for the workers in the city, the color means a break and a rest on top of everything else because holidays are marked on calendar in that color. No one calls Santa Claus "*bbal-gaeng-i*" and everybody looks for red days in the calendar when the new year begins. In short, the color red in Korea does not have any single consistent meaning.

62 | Why is Korea's city nightscape full of red crosses?

This question is actually a combination of two questions put together: why are there so many churches in Korea and why do these churches all have red crosses on top of their roof?

Foreigners who visit Seoul for the first time are deeply intrigued by the red neon crosses that create fascinating scenery at night. Even those who originate from countries that have adopted Christianity much earlier than Korea are astonished by the landscape and realize that the number of crosses in Korea largely outnumbers the number of crosses found in their homeland. The neon crosses that lit up at fixed intervals in between buildings along with the pointed spire is more than enough to portray Korea as the world's largest Christian nation. To be more specific, Korea should be noted as the world's largest protestant nation given the fact that seven of the world's top ten churches and 41 of the world's top 50 churches are all located in Korea.

The quick expansion of Christianity and especially Protestantism in Korea is closely related to Korea's rapid modernization and urbanization, embodying a significant meaning about the geographic aspects of modern Korean society. Although the rapid growth of Korean churches may be seen as God's great blessing, it can also be interpreted as a social and cultural phenomenon which allows us to better understand modern Korean society. Consequently, the growth of Christianity can be explained from the features and the roles fulfilled by the churches within Korean society.

The spread of Christianity actually dates back much earlier than we think. During the 16th century, at the time of the Japanese invasions, the Western priests along with the Japanese Army entered Joseon and practiced minimal missionary work but the actual expansion of Christianity began in the 20th century, with the independence from Japanese imperialism in 1945 followed by the rapid urbanization of the 1960s and the 1970s. For Koreans, Christianity came to serve as a new alternative to the weak national religions such as Buddhism and Cheondogyo[4] which could not be exercised to their full capacity. Moreover, the relief supplies sent by Western churches were not simply regarded as faith to the impoverished generation but as a lifeline. The rapid modernization, too, was based on the civilization of Christianity and shaped it as Korea's religion rather than a Western religion. By becoming a resting place for the confused and tired souls of the cities, the Korean churches created new communities and relationships between people living in the unfamiliar cities. Then it began Korean Christianity's golden era. Having developed

4
Cheondogyo is a traditional Korean religion that began in late Joseon

within such environment and community, Korean churches did indeed struggle with a number of internal problems and difficulties. It is still an undeniable fact that Korea possesses the largest number of Christians and that religion in Korea poses the most influence in the society.

If the above explanation answered the rationale behind the vast number of churches in Korea, it is time for us to explore the reasons why these churches employ neon crosses. Interestingly enough, no one is exactly aware of when the neon crosses began to emerge and there are no such data to explain the phenomenon. Based on some reports, we can assume that since the early 1980s, many churches began to erect crosses on top of their church rooftops. The benefits of neon lights in the night sky are very straightforward (a guiding light for the lost soul being one of them) and a further explanation would not be necessary. Although some argue that the red color applied on crosses symbolizes Christ's blood, it is more likely that the color is chosen so that they can be well spotted at night.

As a matter of fact, it is very unusual to encounter similar neon crosses in other Christian countries. Besides, so many crosses packed so closely together can only be found in graveyards. According to some data, it was a while after the early church periods that crosses were used to symbolize Christian churches. It was only since the 6th century A.D. that the crosses were erected on top of the churches. Perhaps in the future, Korea's neon crosses may also become an important phenomenon in world Christian history.

63 | Why are Korean temples so colorful?

Yes, Korean temples are very colorful and splendid! Their extravagance can be seen in the golden statues of Buddha to *dancheong*, a traditional Korean pattern used in the exteriors of the traditional architectures. Let's take a look at "Iljumun" which is the main gate of Korean temples. Once past Iljumun, we encounter another gate guarded by the Four Devas, or the four heavenly guardians of Buddhism. When closely examined, the Four Devas[5] are painted in bright and vivid colors. Once you enter the precincts of a shrine, it gets even better: the interiors are filled with a more glamorous feast of colors. A foreigner once called such Korean temples a world of hell filled with colors because he thought that they were too much. Well, it all depends on one's personal taste but it definitely raises an intriguing question: Isn't the extravagance of Korean temples contradictory to one of the main teachings of Buddhism, '空'—the principle of emptiness? Buddhism also asserts that colors are transitory and evanescent so why are Korean temples so full of colors? The exquisite embellishment of traditional multicolored paintwork and the beautiful flower patterns decorating Korean temples lead to another question: how are these fancy ornaments relevant to any of the Buddhist teachings?

Simply put, there is a strong relationship between flowers and the enlightenment of Buddha. A lotus flower miraculously blooming in the mud is the most representative symbol of the enlightenment of Buddha. Many statues of Buddha are decorated with lotus flowers and lots of Buddhist temples are dotted with drawn or carved lotus patterns. If you look closely under the eaves of wooden roofs with traditional multicolored paintwork, you will

5
It is enshrined a Devas Statue in the King's Gate when entering the precincts of the temple in Korea. Original Devas was a king of demons that had been worshiped in the religion of ancient India, but became a guardian to protect Buddha and doctrine of Buddhism.

find they have an image of lotus flowers about to burst into a full blossom. In other words, the inflorescence of the lotus symbolizes the enlightenment in which the darkness turns into light. The door gratings of the main shrine at Sudeoksa Buddhist Temple, which is famous for its flower patterns, have the same meaning.

Many statues of Buddha in Korean temples are decorated with gold and the walls ornamented with a lot of beautiful and bright colors unlike Japanese temples decorated in more calm wooden colors.

The beauty of Korean temples is comparable to other royal palaces. It is not just because they are glamorous and flamboyant but because their extravagant colors and patterns symbolize the enlightenment and sublimity of Buddha's world.

Japanese people consider traditional temples as artistic and historical architecture. They also have a distinctive attitude about preserving and fixing old traditional temples: they prefer to leave the old things as they are. In contrast, Koreans are likely to repair and repaint immediately whenever there is any damaged wall or decolorized paintworks. Koreans believe it is important to restore the traditional temples to their original state and in the optimal condition. Nowadays, the government forbids a reckless restoration of the cultural or national properties and treasures but there is still a strong tendency to restore the temples to their old glory in Korea.

In order to fully understand how colors were used differently in Korean temples and Japanese temples, we need to examine the traditional ideologies that informed the temple architectures. We also need to thoroughly consider whether or not these temples were built for artistic or religious purposes. According to the recent data, one of the most famous Japanese temples called

Pyeongdeungwon has been restored to its original state by way of computer graphics. It is surprising to see that some Japanese temples were just as colorful as Korean temples!

64 | Why do Koreans like magpies and dislike crows?

Koreans are very fond of magpies but unfriendly toward crows. Magpies are often associated with the image of hometown or good news whereas the crows remind people of death and graveyards. Such images of these two birds are derived from the black color of the crow that reminds people of the death angel in black dress in Korean folktales. Meanwhile, the magpies appear in Korean folktales and fables as the symbol of good news. It was these magpies that informed the birth of Talhae-wang, the fourth king of Silla and appeared in many temple foundation myths as the messenger of Buddha. They also symbolize good deeds like in the myth about the two estranged lovers who can reunite only every July 7 in lunar year with the help of the magpies forming a bridge over the river that separates them. *Hojakdo*, the very typical genre of Korean folk painting, depicts a tiger and magpies. These images are deeply imprinted in Koreans' minds so they think that the magpie represents Korea. Accordingly, more than 70 local governments have selected magpies as their representative official bird.

On the other hand, crows are considered to be ominous birds, symbolizing death and misfortune. While magpies are the messengers of good news, the crying of the crows is regarded as an omen. Even though the crow, the bird of bad luck, is actually a beneficial one which feeds on harmful insects just like magpies, it has yet to overcome its negative image in Korea. In European Christian cultures, the crow normally symbolizes evil and sin as well. It is frightening to recall the image of a flock of crows which appear in Alfred Hitchcock's films. In other cultures, the same bird is regarded as the symbol of creation or wisdom. In Aesop's "The Crow and the Pitcher," the crow is depicted as a wise bird.

Koreans' perception about the magpie and crows has no connection to the actual characteristic of the birds themselves. Like the two sides of the same coin, crows symbolize both good and evil but only the latter in Korean culture. The fate of magpies, however, is rather inconsistent to today's Koreans who are not that familiar with magpies anymore. They have become troublesome as they increase in numbers. They build their nests on telephone poles and cause a great deal of property damage due to short-circuit failures. The workers of Korean electric power corporations have the legal right to shoot down magpies and destroy their nests that used to be considered the symbols of good luck. Magpies and crows are still flying around Korea but their fate does not seem like what it used to be.

65 | Why are Koreans interested in other's blood types?

When foreigners visit Korea, they immediately realize that Korean people have a vast interest in each other's blood type and are strongly convinced that it is a good indication of one's personality. The public awareness of the correlation between one's blood type and personality dates back to a book called *Blood Type Anthropology* written by a Japanese author in 1971. There had been people who attempted to reveal the correlation between blood types, human types and physiological characteristics even before the book but it was Japan where such correlation became a sensational hit and eventually spread to Korea. In fact, Koreans and Japanese are the only people who relate blood types to personality although there is no conclusive correlation whatsoever between the two.

Then why are there so many people who determine other's personality based on blood types? This is an intriguing fact which is worth our attention. What makes people believe in the personality of the different blood types? Such hasty generalization based on blood types has been prevailing in Korean society and especially on the Internet. Based on the blood type theory, people with A types are timid, B types are playboys (or even that they are better at conjugal relationships), and ABs are unpredictable. It seems absurd to categorize people's personality based on different blood types but people often use this information to determine or predict the outcome of their relationships.

Given the advent of an advertisement which recommends a particular learning method that fits different blood types, an anthropological study of blood types and their personalities may soon become one of Korea's major cultural products. It seems that this kind of phenomenon is based on people's needs to judge others easily and quickly to relieve anxieties in relationship.

66 | Why is the 4th floor written as "F" in Korean buildings?

In most buildings with elevators, the fourth floors are usually marked as F or not marked at all because the Korean pronunciation of number '4 (*sa*)' is the same as that of the Chinese letter '死 (*sa*)' meaning death. Although it could be simply a superstition to say the pronunciation of a certain number is related to death, most people are still reluctant to press a number 4 button when they are on the elevator. Foreigners may be curious about the mark F which comes from an English word 'Four.' So there it is: most of the fourth floors in Korea are marked as F floor after the English word 'Four.' The cultural differences are clearly shown when Koreans do not care about 3 and 9 which are often considered as taboos in other countries. Americans tend to avoid number 13 because it reminds them of Judas who betrayed Jesus. For Japanese, the pronunciation of 9 is similar to that of 'hardship' so it is not regarded as a good number. There is no empirical evidence to prove the influence of the number taboos but people still seem very concerned about them. In case of Korea, even satellites skip number four. The government is planning to send the 5th satellite right after the third one. This is based on the belief that people would prefer to avoid ominous things in uncertain and dangerous situations even if they are very trivial.

Another intriguing point about numbers is the opinion that Koreans were actually fond of number 4. The researchers who support this argument claim that Koreans' dislike of number 4 began from the Japanese colonial period. They argue that Japanese avoided number 4 because its pronunciation (*si* or *shi*) reminded people of death and thus Koreans have also adopted this idea since then. Traditionally Koreans followed the *sasin-gwannyeom* which indicates cardinal points and were heavily influenced by Chinese culture that actually preferred number 4. For these assumptions, it is still uncertain how Korean people came to shun number 4 but one thing is clear: Japan and Korea are the only countries that sidestep number 4. The F floors in Korea's elevators still remain an enigma for most foreigners.

67 | Why are there so many apartments in Korea?

Korea, most definitely, is the land of apartments or so to speak the "republic of apartments." Foreigners who arrive in Seoul may be surprised by the myriad of neon crosses at night and are yet again surprised by the number of large-sized apartments in the morning. A French geographer who began his research after being astonished by the vast number of apartments in Korea entitled his book, *The Republic of Apartments*.[6] According to some statistics, Korea's total population living in the apartments outnumbers any other nationality by a large margin. Approximately 52% of the entire population live in the apartments. The supply of apartments also largely overwhelms the supply of residential houses. If this trend continues, some speculate that almost the entire nation may soon live in apartments and that residential houses may become extinct. Should this truly happen in the near future, "republic of apartment Korea" may be a more suitable name for the country.

Although it is hard to find any specific records, the first

6
Valerie Gelezeau
(2007). *The Republic of Apartments*. Seoul: Humanitas.

apartment constructed in Korea was built in the 30s whereas the first large-scale residential apartment complex called, Mapo Apartment, was constructed in 1964. It only took about 50 years for half of the entire population to live in the new residential apartments. It is also notable to see how rapidly a large number of apartments were built in such a short span of time. The new housing and urban policies were implemented in the 1960s in order to accommodate the rapid influx of population migrating to the capital city. It was not until the 1970s that the large-scale apartment complexes prioritizing the economic feasibility and strategic conveniences emerged rapidly. The first experimental apartment of its kind was built in Yeoido and soon became the standard for all other apartments. Also, these apartments that most Koreans saw as Western and therefore a better lifestyle became the top investment in the 1980s. The population continued to migrate to Seoul in the 1990s and called for a new town development and urban planning businesses.

The apartment complexes in Korea have become an integral part of people's everyday daily lives in the 21st century. In order to become middle class men or women in the city, one has to own an apartment and those who already owned one would soon dream of living in a much comfortable and spacious apartment. The French geographer states that, "asking Koreans why they live in apartments is equivalent to asking them why they live." This statement alone exhibits what apartments mean to Korean people. Korea's argument that apartments were constructed due to the small land mass is logical to a certain extent but there must be some other reasons since the number of apartments in Korea outnumbers those in other small countries such as the Netherlands that boast of a much higher population density.

According to some scholars, the apartments in Korea were not simply constructed to efficiently accommodate the large population in a small country but as a result of the development policies imposed by the government and conglomerates in the process of modernization and urbanization. What will the future of Korean apartments look like? Currently, the numerous development businesses to build new cities and towns reemphasize that the apartments in Korea are recognized more as an investment product rather than a place of living. Accordingly, the houses that urbanites live in will sooner or later be replaced by more apartments. Koreans in the 21st century are fast becoming the modern nomads of apartments.

68 | Why does the oldest person usually pay for everyone at a restaurant?

In Korea, it is usually the oldest person who wins the bill and this may also seem strange to many foreigners. Koreans are still influenced by Confucian philosophy which is very prevalent even in today's contemporary Korean society. As already mentioned several times, the concept of *jangyuyuseo*, which means 'elders first,' automatically establishes a strict vertical order based on one's age and thus the younger ones are expected to obey and respect the elders. Such respect, however, comes with a price because the older ones have duties to take care of the younger ones. To this extent, the oldest person among the group becomes the first candidate to pay for everyone when dining out. If the oldest person does not treat the younger ones to meals, he or she may get an image of being a mean and petty senior and end up losing the respect of the younger people. It seems very unfair and one-sided phenomenon but we must also remember that the older person hasn't always been the oldest one in a group. It goes around and the young ones who were always treated to meals by the older ones will eventually become the oldest in a group and return the same kind of favor that they have received when they were young. The easiest way to understand Korea's bill-paying culture is by remembering to get treated by older people and then return the favor to younger ones.

X

TRADITIONS
& CUSTOMS

69 | What's the meaning of Seollal?

Seollal, or New Year's Day, is the first day of the new year and thus has a special meaning. Different cultures have different ways to calculate the passage of time and seasons and the beginning of a new cycle is significant in every culture. Koreans, however, celebrate the beginning of a new year twice every year, once based on the solar year and once based on the lunar year. Koreans follow the cycle of solar calendars officially but Seollal in the lunar year is still observed following the tradition. In fact, the lunar New Year's Day is much more celebrated as a major national family holiday. It may seem strange to celebrate the first day twice so the total number of holidays for two Seollal seasons became a lot shorter than in the past.

In the past in Korea, people used to pray for a successful harvest year and good fortunes and health for the family members and townspeople during Seollal. They start Seollal with an ancestral worship in order to strengthen the bond between the living and the dead. As the first service of a new year, people prepare most special food and drinks for their guests. They even have special names for new dresses they buy for their children on this very special day: *seolbim*. In the past, new cloth for new dresses was very expensive so children eagerly waited for Seollal to get their hands on the long-waited new outfits. Once they change into a newly made or purchased dress, they would bow to their ancestors first and then to the elders in order of seniority. The elders who have received the bow gave blessings and some monetary gifts, another reason for children's anticipation and excitement for Seollal season. It would be unimaginable to think of the New

Year's Day without these cash gifts and you can almost hear children tallying up in their head how much they would earn after each bowing.

Another important tradition of Seollal is a rice cake soup called *tteokguk*. Koreans believe that eating a bowl of rice-cake soup is a sign of becoming a year older. After the ancestral worship and the bowing, all family members and relatives gather around to play several games played only on New Year's Day. Among those, a game called *yunnori* is most popular and most apt for cramped city life since other games like *neolttwigi*[1] or flying kites require large open spaces.

In agrarian society Seollal was not just a holiday for one family but a celebration to wish for the peace and prosperity of the whole village. Therefore, people prepared the town *gut*[2] and *nongak*[3] performance and went around the whole town to exorcise evil spirits and pray for a good harvest. Such traditions, too, faded away a long time ago and only a few villages near coastlines and on islands still prepare *gut* and *nongak* on Seollal. In today's industrialized society, people still pray for peace and prosperity but only with their close relatives and a much more personal and quiet ancestral worship service. Despite these changes, however, people continue to anticipate Seollal since it is still a day children receive money and one of the longest holiday breaks from work for adults.

1
It is a play enjoyed by Korean young women in New Year's Day. Having hay in the middle of the long plate, it looks like a seesaw, but two people stand, instead of seating, at the end of the plate and jump one by one.

2
Gut is a service for god directed by a shaman to pray for the adjustment of one's fate.

3
It is music played in rural village to entertain the people when working together in a group.

70 | What does Chuseok mean to Koreans?

The translation of the Chinese characters composing of the word Chuseok means 'moon in autumn'. Chuseok falls on the 15th of August in the lunar calendar. The dates differ each year in the Gregorian calendar but it is usually somewhere in the middle of autumn (September or October) and always lands on a full moon. Chuseok is also called Hangawi, which means "mid-autumn festival" in pure Korean. The Chuseok holiday is considered the most beautiful time of year; the weather is cool, not cold, the skies are clear and the leaves are changing throughout the country. The best time of the year doesn't mean only good weather. In previous agrarian societies, the harvest for farmers came at this time and Chuseok represented a period of plenty. Grains, ripe fruit and berries are brought in from the felids. Chuseok is the harvest season and the time to remember ancestors.

During Chuseok, people prepare and share the newly harvested foods and perform *jesa*. Here sharing food doesn't mean simply sitting and eating at the table. Chuseok is also a time to eat sacred food that brings luck and happiness to those who eat together. The food offered to ancestors during *jesa* receives the ancestors' blessings and becomes sacred food. After the food is offered and the ancestors 'eat', the people can begin eating.

The most symbolic food of Chuseok is *songpyeon*, half-moon shaped rice cakes. In China, the typical harvest festival food is full-moon cakes, while in Korea it is half-moon shaped rice cakes. According to the region, the size and shape can be slightly different, but the basic recipe is *songpyeon* filled with sesame seeds or beans.

Of course, games are also an important part of Hangawi and they differ from region to region. As it is the end of farming season, many different games are played throughout the country to celebrate all the hard work that has been done over the year. Farmers' music is played. Korean wrestling, cow and turtle games take place. Cows play[4] a main role in the games and they show the very essence of Chuseok.

One more thing that should be mentioned about Chuseok is the "massive movement of people" which also happens during Seollal. This refers to people traveling back to their hometowns. Just 30 or 40 years ago, 70% of the population lived in villages, but now it is just the opposite. Millions of people have left their hometowns to move to the big cities. For Koreans it is still very important to go back home for Chuseok. This is a holiday to spend time with their families and pay respect to dead ancestors in their hometowns. At this time all trains and buses are fully booked. When children, who now work and live in the city, go back home they can show off their success and make their family proud.

But as time goes by, the meaning of one's hometown is also changing. In patriarchal Confucian society, women worked hard to prepare food for the *jesa* rituals and to treat guests graciously during Chuseok. Nowadays women are less willing to 'slave' away for the holidays. People talk about the quarrels that happen between spouses before and after Chuseok. In the past, only train stations and bus terminals were crowded, but now the international airport is full of Koreans, who want to have vacation during the holidays rather than celebrate back home. Many are concerned about what direction Korean Chuseok is headed in and whether or not old traditions are being lost to new conveniences.

4
It is a traditional Korean folk play. The player would make the shape of cow, and bring it to every house in the village to pray for peace and good harvest in the year. The host would invite the visitors to the house and serve them food and drink.

71 | Why do Koreans become one year old as soon as they are born?

There are two ways of counting age in Korea. That is why there are many confusing situations of asking one's age twice.

The first way is counting years and the second way is counting birthdays (starting from the first birthday party, called *dol*, which is equivalent to the international age system). By saying one year, two years, and so forth in Korea, not the actual number of years a person has been living in being counted, but the number of new years a person welcomed after a baby was born, or the number of years a baby has experienced, and saying one *dol*, two *dol* means the actual duration of life, how many years passed since a baby was born. If a baby is born now in 2015, the baby becomes one year old, because the baby has an experience of living in 2015. When the new 2016 year comes, no matter how many days passed since one's birth, the baby automatically becomes two years old, because the baby has lived in another year. But after a baby's actual date of birth, after one year, the baby will have the first birthday party (in another word, *dol*). Because of this system, there can be some amazing cases. For example, if a baby is born on December 31 in 2015, the baby is one year old, but the next day when 2016 comes, one becomes two years old. Usually the common way is counting years, but according to the system, the *dol* way of counting is more common, which is called '*man na-i*', counting age in full, like in many other countries. But, in many related and local systems, there is no clear differentiation between '*man na-i*' and '*yeon na-i*' (counting years, when a person lived in), which can be confusing to foreigners. If there is no additional reference, most of the time '*man na-i*' is meant.

Sometimes, people explain that Koreans become one year old as soon as they are born, because they count ten months (to be exact forty weeks) of the time spent inside the mother's stomach during pregnancy. This explanation is not right because when the first birthday party *dol* is held those ten months are not counted. So, the reason why the child becomes one year old at the moment the baby is born is because the baby meets the first year of the one's life.

Counting the age of a child by *dol*, we suppose that *dol* means 'coming back of one year'. This unit of *dol* is not used only for counting a child's age, but also for counting a group's age.[5]

There is a tradition in Korea to eat *tteokguk* (rice cake soup) every New Year, which means you are one year older. This tradition shows that the Korean way of counting age depends on how many years the person welcomes, not the actual duration of life. In Western countries, the age shows the period of how many years a person has lived since one was born, but in Korea it is a way to count the number of years the person experienced.

The meaning of age to Koreans is as special as the way of counting it. According to one's age, there are regulations of what a person can or should do. Certain types of movies can be seen from fifteen or eighteen years (*man na-i*) and those nineteen (*man na-i*) and older can legally buy. When a person reaches a certain age, it is mandatory to quit his job, no matter of one's capabilities. Of course, there are differences, dependents on the field. Apart from these legal procedures, there are some cultural norms, which cause certain actions, depending on age. If the person is over thirty and not married yet, people call him or her an old bachelor or old maid (*nochonggak* or *nocheonyeo* in Korean) showing that the chance to they can marry is very low. There is also an

5
For example, the company becomes 50 dol tomorrow means that tomorrow will be the 50th anniversary of the establishment of the company.

expression "You should pay the price of your age", which also shows the relation of age and certain cultural norms that have to be accomplished according to age.

Actually, the importance of age begins with the very moment when two people meet for the first time. The first thing to do here is to find out the age difference between each other. According to the age, the way in which you refer to someone is decided, as well as, the whole relationship. Because of these cultural norms, asking each other's age in Korea is common. For example, according to the other person's age, he can call me in many different ways: "Teacher Kim", "Mister Kim Young Hoon" (Kim Young Hoon *ssi*), "Kim *hyoung*", "Young Hoon *hyoung*" (older brother) or just Young Hoon.

72 | Why do Koreans have seaweed soup on their birthday?

Eating a special meal on a special day is very common in all cultures. The custom of eating seaweed soup (*miyeokguk*) on one's birthday originates from childbirth rituals in Korea. The first food a mother takes after her first childbirth is seaweed soup and it remains as the main dish until she is fully recovered. Koreans eat seaweed soup on their birthday to remember the hardship their mothers had gone through during the pregnancy. It acts as a medium to link the mother and the child, thus differentiating the seaweed soup served on birthdays from other foods that are served on a daily basis.

Then, why is it that Korean mothers are served with seaweed

soup after childbirth? There are two possible reasons to explain this phenomenon. First, seaweed provides an abundant supply of iodine which helps to compensate for the loss of blood during childbirth and allows mothers to quickly regain their loss of blood and her health. The value of seaweed soup has not been proven through scientific experiments but from a long period of valuable experience. It is traditionally said that mothers were served with seaweed soup after whales were spotted eating seaweed after giving birth: This explanation is highly unlikely, however, since it is not easy to spot whales eating seaweed or confirm the fact that they only consume seaweed after giving birth.

The second possible reason is the slippery texture of seaweed. Fundamentally, giving birth describes the process of a baby coming out from the mother's womb and the hope for various substances, including the placenta, to be safely excreted after birth are symbolically sublimated in the slippery properties of seaweed.

Whether or not these two possible reasons are true, the wisdom of our ancestors consuming seaweed soup after giving birth has provided mothers and children with abundant nutrition. As a matter of fact, the practice of eating seaweed soup was so accepted as a fact of life that it was considered taboo to bargain the price of seaweed or to fold them in half. Considering the difficulties of pregnancy and the high infant mortality, it is easy to understand why some food served to mothers after childbirth had a rather significant meaning to it.

Seaweed soup has undergone a gradual transition from such childbirth customs to a representative food served on birthdays. Consequently, if one says that he or she was not able to eat seaweed soup on their birthday, it means that event was not properly celebrated and the involved person deserves other's pity and sympathy. Also, those who scored poorly on tests or have failed to accomplish their goals use the expression "I ate seaweed soup" to express their disappointment and grief. Such a metaphor emphasizes the slipperiness of the seaweed to describe the unfortunate situation. It should be noted that this is simply an expression and that those who score poorly on their examination did not actually eat seaweed.

73 | Why are most Korean names composed of three syllables?

Most names in Korea are composed of three syllables. Sometimes, there are other names which are longer, or names made of a single syllable, but they are not very common. Moreover, this three-syllable composition of a name follows the Chinese tradition of making names. The first syllable is the surname which represents family, the second represents the generation and is the same for all clan members who were born in the same generation, and the third one is created especially for the name holder.

A long time ago, before Chinese characters were introduced into Korea, people had other names, very different from nowadays. In the history books we can easily see names like Hyeokgeose, Suro, Eulji, Isabu, Geochilbu, Sadaham, Gaesomun. They are not made of Chinese characters like today; they are composed of pure Korean.

With the wide spread of Chinese characters after the Unified Silla, most names gradually started changing according to the Chinese pattern.

Before that, there was no differentiation between the surname and first name. Only in the Three Kingdoms era (57 BC- 668), the notion of surname emerged among the upper class, but it didn't spread to ordinary people, and they still used only first names.

Despite having a surname, there was a thing called *kwan*[6] or the notion of clan, which emerged near the end of the Silla dynasty. Usually the name of the clan originated from the name of the region where the family was coming from. The creation of a separate surname was a way to show the superiority of the clan. According to the surname and clan name, the relationship between people could be tracked. If the surname and clan were the same, this could be considered as belonging to the same family. But, as there were cases when the surname or clan were granted by the king, or just copied from others and used as one's own, we cannot definitely say that having the same surname and clan name showed real family relations.

A tendency to follow the Chinese way of making names became common with the wide spread of Chinese culture. Approximately from the middle of the Goryeo dynasty (912-1392), almost all names were composed of Chinese characters. The notion of a syllable, representing generation, which was mentioned above, appeared at the same period. Family members of the same generation have a common syllable in their names. For example, in "Young Hoon", "Young Joo", "Young Gyu"; 'Young' was used as the syllable which represented a generation. In my father's generation "Hwan" was used as a generation syllable, and in my children's generation "Seop" was used for this purpose.

In societies, like the Joseon, where ancestor worshiping ceremonies were of a great importance, the surname, and generation mark also played an important role, because filial

6
It is also called Bonkwan. This concept has a very important meaning in traditional Korean society. The statements like "A person doesn't know his/her roots" or "He/She has no roots whatsoever" means that a person doesn't even know his/her own ancestors. Koreans find these expressions very insulting.

piety, collective identity and group solidarity were common ethic norms. The group solidarity was very well shown in names, where surname and syllable, representing generation, took two syllables out of three. This tradition is still alive nowadays. We can even say that the structure of Korean names is the fundamental element in Korean culture, which shows the collective mind of Koreans the best. As two syllables of three are already decided while creating a name for a child, Korean names often lack creativity and originality.

The traditional culture of creating names suffered during the Japanese colonization. There was a policy to assimilate Koreans with Japanese by destroying their cultural roots. This policy also included forcing Koreans to change their names into Japanese ones.

For example, the syllable *ja*, which means son, was a common syllable of a Japanese female name during that period. As many people possessed newly created Japanese names, even now, the most common syllable in Korean female names is meant to be *ja*, like Young Ja, Jeong Ja, Sun Ja, and so on. This example shows how strong Japanese influence was during that time, and that Japanese colonization still remains as a painful scar in Korean history.

After gaining independence, a new tendency of creating pure Korean names emerged. More and more people tend to give their children pure Korean names with no Chinese characters or Japanese tradition.

After the establishment of the government, in September 1947 the first pure Korean name 'Geum Nan Sae'[7] (Keum Nan-sae) appeared in the family register. There were different campaigns of language associations, encouraging people to use more pure

7

He is a conductor who won a prize at the 5th Karajan International Conducting Contest in 1977 the first for a Korean. His name, Geum Nan Sae meaning 'birds flying in the air', is purely made uses only Hangeul letters. His father Geum Su Hyeon played a pioneering role in giving Hangeul names to his children, including Geum No San and Geum Nu Ree.

Korean names. These campaigns had very fruitful results, and many pure Korean names were created. Recently, there is one more new tendency of using surnames of both parents because of the issue of gender equality. In this case, my name is supposed to be changed to Kim Lee Young Hoon.

74 | Why doesn't a Korean wife take the surname of her husband after marriage?

In the USA, when people get married, a wife usually takes the surname of a husband. In Italy, Great Britain or other European countries, there is the same custom, but it is not mandatory. It is also possible to have the surname of a husband after marriage, or, like in Russia, spouses can decide whether to take the surname of a husband or keep her surname. Also, it is possible not to choose between two surnames, but make a new one by combining two of them, which is common in Taiwan.

What is the origin of the tradition of a wife taking the surname of a husband in Western countries? In most cases, it is the influence of patriarchy. Humans are born as individuals, but socially they are born as members of a family. The way of becoming a member of a family is either through blood ties or marriage. But, in the case of a patriarchal household system, the family line goes from father to son, and it is necessary for a woman to take the surname of her husband in order to become a member of the family.

But why in the patriarchal and male-centered traditional Korean society, did a wife not take the surname of a husband? It might seem very unreasonable and strange. Is it because there was some kind of equality between men and women, and women were not forced to take the surname of a husband? In the male dominated society of the Joseon dynasty (1392-1910), the reason was just the opposite. There were cases, among ordinary people when women didn't even get any name, and among the number of *yangban* women's name and surname were also not of a great importance. Even though daughters were biological children, they were not considered as members of the family, and their names were not written in the family register. Women during the Joseon dynasty were considered more like an almost invisible part of society.

Like this, the tradition of women not taking the surname of a husband, or better to say, not being able to take it, originates from discrimination of women. But, the position of women in Korean history was not always like that during the Joseon dynasty. Just before Joseon, there wasn't female discrimination in inheriting properties or performing ancestors' worshiping rituals. The concept of the paternal family line was settled only at the end of Joseon dynasty. Before that, the mother and father had equally important roles in the family. If we consider the facts that during the Goryeo dynasty (918-1392) women could remarry, or, in the kingdom of Silla, there were even queens, we can see that the women's position has been constantly changing throughout Korean history. And it is changing now, as well. Nowadays, there is a new phenomenon of taking both the mother's and father's surnames, which can be considered as a sign of the shifting role of women in Korean society.

XI

KOREAN IDENTITY

75 | What is the origin of 'Korea' as a country name?

An official country name is created by the nation's law. Korea is officially named Daehanminguk in Korean and the Republic of Korea in English according to the law. The nation's official name, however, is not always the same as the one in popular usage. Korea is generally referred to as Hanguk by Koreans, rather than Daehanminguk. *'Dae! Han-min-guk'*, chanted by Koreans cheering for their soccer team during the 2002 World Cup, is the nation's official name. However, Koreans generally use the term Hanguk to refer their country. *'Dae'* of Daehanminguk literally means 'large', but is not appropriate to represent Korea considering its relatively small number of people and the size of territory. *'Dae'* actually reflects Korean's national pride as the name was made when Korea gained independence from Japan's colonial administration.[1] Naming the nation has its own history. Today's name of 'Korea' originated from the Goryeo dynasty, which lasted from 935 AD to 1391 AD Goryeo, which boasted unexcelled selections of celadon pottery, was known to the Western world around the 12th century and the country has been called Korea since then. Korea remains divided, so its name could be changed if the two Koreas, the Republic of Korea and the Democratic People's Republic of Korea, are reunified. Maybe then could its new name be the United States of Korea?

1
As Japan lost in World War II Korea regained sovereignty and celebrated its freedom from Japan after a 35-year period of colonial rule.

76 | Is Korea an ethnically homogenous country?

To the older generations, the above question might be considered sacrilege because Koreans' sense of nationalism is stronger than many other nations. Anyone who casts doubts on such belief may become a target of social outcry in Korea. Despite Korea's strong sense of nationalism, the number of international marriages and naturalization of foreigners continues to increase very rapidly and has begun to cast doubts on whether or not the new generations of Koreans will maintain the pride of previous generations. The increasing number of single farmers marrying foreign women, especially from South-East Asia, along with the interracial children from these marriages, is beginning to pose imminent social issues in Korean society.

One of the most notable problems has been the definition of Koreans as a homogenous race and Korea as a one-blood nation in Korean textbooks. Based on this definition, Tae-seong Johnson, who is a half-black, half-Korean born in Korea and thus can only speak Korean, would be considered a non-Korean and a foreigner. It may be true that Korea is relatively more homogenous than other countries, but it is hard to call the blood of a particular race "pure". In other words, various historical data show that since ancient times people from China, Vietnam, Mongolia, Japan and many other countries settled in Korea for many centuries until now. This is all to say that Koreans' strong conviction in "pure blood" or one-bloodline is in fact a mere misconception and far from the truth. It is thus important to think about how such belief emerged and became such an important value in Korea. The idea of Koreans being a homogenous race is a relatively recent

The period from the
4th century to the
mid-7th century.

concept. In the Three Kingdoms period[2], Gokuryeo, Baekje, and Silla were very hostile to each other, so how or why did Koreans come to believe in such a strong ethnic nationalism based on homogeneity? There may be two reasons, which are as follows: first, Japan's annexation of Korea and a long colonial history resulted in the emergence of a Korean nationalism that allows for people's unity and a collective desire to maintain their national identity under threat by a foreign power; and second, Korea was in desperate need to rebuild itself after the liberation immediately followed by the Korean War, so the nationalist fervor was once again revitalized under the Park Jeong-hee[3] regime. At the time, the state constantly reminded people that each and everyone born in this land had a duty to restore the nation. The Korean Pledge of Allegiance which urges people to devote their hearts and souls to the nation and its success very well exemplifies Korea's strong emphasis on nationalism.

Even after Korea was liberated from Japan, they were still devastated by poverty and war and felt helpless. The revitalization of the Korean economy and rebuilding of the nation thus paralleled the recovery of the Korean people's national pride. Therefore, one's individual happiness was secondary to the nation's development and progress and personal sacrifices seemed like a very natural and reasonable social responsibility. The Park Jeong-hee regime instilled and promoted Korean nationalism by using the images of patriotic heroes and heroines who gave up their lives to challenge the foreign powers and protect the nation.

Today, people often criticize Korean nationalism for being a very male-centered and militant ideology that was used by Park's regime to validate its authority and power. Park's legacy of Korean nationalism is still very much a part of Korean culture and at times acts as a means to mobilize the nation. For example, the Korean national soccer team is called, "Taegeuk Warriors," who are like those patriotic heroes and heroines from the Park Jeong-hee era. Although times have changed, Korean nationalism still seems to be a fundamental and everlasting element of Korean culture. However, it would become very difficult to classify the new generations who have grown up under a totally new social environment. How would they identify with those Korean descendants in Central Asia? What about North Koreans? Would they be foreigners as currently defined by international law or would they be considered as South Koreans? How would naturalized foreigners and their children, as well as interracial families, also change the definition of the Korean race? These questions have encouraged the younger generations to approach the issues of Korean identity, nation, and nationalism with a more open-mind and with a global perspective. Benedict Anderson, a famous historian, suggested that a nation is an "imagined community". Accordingly, the question we have to ask ourselves is not about the definitions of Korean ethnicity or nationalism but how we should redefine the term "ethnic race".

77 | What does Baekdusan Mountain mean to Koreans?

Baekdusan Mountain, which even appears in the Korean national anthem, occupies a very special place in the hearts of the people of the two Koreas. Meaning 'white-headed peak', the name Baekdu originated from the mountain's highest peak, which makes the mountain outstand all year around. The Baekdu-daegan chain of the mountain forms the backbone of the Korean peninsula. Baekdusan Mountain begins at its peak with 2,744 meters (9,003 feet) of height and stretches to the southern part of the Korean peninsula. As mountains cover more than 70 percent of Korea, Koreans worshipped Sansin (Mountain God) as part of religion. In this regard, Koreans refer to the highest Baekdusan Mountain as a holy mountain in which Sansin resides. The Korean geomantic principles of 'Pungsu', under which people believe auspicious landscape determines one's fortunes, also made Baekdu a holy mountain.

Korea is a hilly and mountainous region. Baekdusan Mountain's long-winding ridges creates a distinct landscape and a unique psychological environment. Some believe Korea's land is economically inefficient because it has a large portions of hilly areas that make it difficult for farming. Is that really true? According to the *National Geographic* in 1945, if Korea's hilly terrains are spread out like a pancake, it would be large enough to cover the whole Earth. The combined land size of South and North Korea amounts to that of the UK and Korea's 5,000 islands and 4,000 mountains create regional diversity, so whether the nation's land is vast or not would be meaningless. From a cultural anthropologist's view, regional diversity created by mountains is an interesting subject to study. Cheonji Lake on top of Baekdusan Mountain with the white peak of the mountain casting its reflection is a sacred and magnificent sight for Koreans. For Koreans, Baekdusan Mountain is not just a place of geographical meaning but the site of their ancestral origin.

78 | What is *jokbo*?

Jokbo is a Korean genealogical record equivalent to the family tree. *Jokbo* was once highly valued, but today few Koreans have ever read their *jokbo*. It traces back the family members and ancestors, but not every family member is listed on it because it was rooted in the patriarchal family system. Some females were listed in *jokbo* as spouses, but not in detail. It also registered sons of concubines. Throughout Korea's history, a rigid class system and monarchy existed, so the bloodline proved one's wealth and power. For this reason, *jokbo*, which revealed their bloodline and social status, was of great significance. The *jokbo* of a king's family has the longest history. Tracing a king's family tree was conducted at the national level. The practice of writing family registry was spread among upper class and even ordinary people afterwards.

Jokbo was written as following orders. The origins and background of the family were first included in *jokbo*. The next covered information of progenitors. Next came the locations of progenitors' tombs and it listed family members' birthday, office positions, contributions and so on. *Jokbo* ends with a family tree. It drew clear lines between legitimate and illegitimate children, males and females. The publication of *jokbo* traces back to the Goryeo period. The *Goryeosa* or *History of Goryeo*, noted the upper class highly regarded family registry but *jokbo* during the Goryeo period has not been found yet. *Jokbo* certified family honor so the upper class without *jokbo* could be descended into the lower class and faced discrimination. For this reason, some even falsified their *jokbo*, bribing to have their *jokbo* changed. *Jokbo* written in the 18th and 19th century exaggerated the origin and office positions of the members to elevate the status of their family. The release of *jokbo* became widespread during the period of Japanese colonialism as was demonstrated by the fact that *jokbo* topped the list among publications. This shows family registry was highly regarded during this period. Things have changed to the point where *jokbo* is now unfamiliar to a majority of Koreans. Rather than family line, individual talent and performance is more valued in today's society. The practice of wealth inheritance still permeates the society, but not as serious as before. *Jokbo* no longer plays a role in dividing social class but those associated with power elites still exercise their influence over the national events like elections. The meaning of *jokbo* has changed and even a digitized version of *jokbo* is released today.

79 | Why do Koreans hesitate to adopt children?

Korea has the highest number of orphans sent abroad for adoptions while the number of domestic adoptions is ranked one of the lowest in the world. These statistics reveal some of the fundamental structures of Korean consciousness and value systems. Korea is ranked as the 6th nation to send highest number of children to other countries for adoption since 1953, after the Korean War. This is very ironic given that Korea is the 11th biggest economic power in the world. Why are Korean children being sent to foreign countries for adoption? Why do Koreans in general seem reluctant to adopt orphans? Simply put, Koreans tend to be very sensitive about the so-called "pure blood" which is based on the traditional patriarchal concept. When an unmarried mother bears a child, the child becomes an unacknowledged bastard shunned by society. Illegitimate children have nowhere to go so the only option for them is to be sent abroad for an adoption. Ironically, Korea has the lowest birth rate in the world. The government encourages childbirth and tries to provide incentives to boost the low birth rate but most of those children given up for adoption are still sent to other countries partly as a result of poor reception in Korea.

Most of the orphans given up for adoption belong to unmarried women. However, it is not true that there are more children from the disabled or unmarried women in Korea compared to other countries. Some statistics show that Korea has the least number of unmarried single mothers among OECD countries but foreign country adoption continues to grow because of traditional Korean values stressing the importance of "pure blood" or bloodlines. No societies would actually encourage or affirm unmarried women to give birth but in Korea, not only the society but even the government discourages the birth of illegitimate children. Korea has almost no welfare policies for single unmarried mothers. Those women who had no choice but to give up their children are condemned by the society as sinners. In short, Korea's history of foreign adoption is the history of the forgotten people that should be explored and discussed openly by people and the government. A plethora of unmarried mothers give up their own children because they lack financial means and because of the social stigma attached to the fatherless and single mothers' children. Given the situation, implementing appropriate welfare policies for the single and the handicapped mothers seems to be the most efficient way to reduce foreign country adoptions. Furthermore, both the state support and the new perception on the value of pure blood and children are necessary to encourage domestic adoption. It is the patriarchal traditions that stigmatize fatherless or single-mother children as bastards, abandoned not only by their mothers but also from their country and people.

80 | What is *han*?

Koreans are said to have *han*, a feeling of sorrow, oppression, unavenged injustice, and isolation. The foreign media and their editorials note that *han* is partly attributed to the success of Korean athletes on the global stage. They argue *han* feelings of frustration and agony contributed to Korean baseball player better performance. What role does *han* play for Korean players? What is the definition of *han*? Are Koreans people of *han*? These are important questions to be answered in order to read the mind of Koreans.

Let's define what *han* is. *Han* has a complex meaning, hard to truly explain. It is a collective feeling of sorrow, regret, grief, resentment and isolation in the face of overwhelming odds. It is also an obstinate urge to take revenge to right the wrong.

So is *han* a national cultural trait displayed only by Koreans? To understand the aspects of *han*, it is necessary to examine historical and cultural backgrounds. Some claim *han* is Korea's unique cultural trait but careful approach is required in comprehending this. In fact, Korea's ancient literatures and traditional art are filled with humor and wit, not *han*.

The examples are the story of Chunhyang and Shim-cheong, which describe a tragic and painful life in a humorous manner. The Hahoe mask dance is also the case. Its main themes are social divide among classes but it does not contain *han* feeling. *Han* is found nowhere in rhythmical *pansori* music as well. Then is why *han* believed to be Korea's cultural trait?

Scholars say *han* feeling traces back to the Japanese colonial period. Japan deprived Koreans of their nation, triggering Koreans to have frustration and grief. During the colonial period, Korea's community culture based on *shinmyeong* was oppressed. Instead, songs about Koreans ill-fate to give in Japan became popular. Japan forced Koreans into believing it is their fate to be under the Japanese occupation and Koreans with no abilities to protest had to accept it. *Han* may come from the Koreans' feelings of resentment and sorrow over the deprivation of their nation.

A famous Korean singer Jo Yong-pil (Cho Yong-pil) has a song titled 500 years of *han* whose lyrics includes the term '*han*'. His mournful singing style and lyrics are deeply embedded in the minds of Korean middle and old-aged people. Nothing would be more appropriate in defining the term *han* than by the describing adversity and frustration during the Japanese colonial rule and dictatorship experienced by them.

Those who could not educate children due to poverty have *han*. Those who lost their beloved ones have *han*. Those who lost their lives in the battle also have *han*. People with such experiences are bound by *han*, gaining sympathy from others. However, such experience is not confined to Koreans. If such events fuel *han* feeling, Jewish people would have the most *han* feelings considering their several thousand years of sufferings caused by having no national rights. And Tibetans would be the people of *han* given that their government is in exile in India. All in all, Koreans traditionally have had humorous characteristics and this *han* feeling came to exist among Koreans largely because of their specific historical experiences including the foreign invasions, and Korean War and the consequent division of the country in 1950s.

Policies during the Japanese colonial rule, ordinary people's hardship from strict class system and people's literature all made *han* feeling became widespread. The more people express *han*, the more *han*-related terms were coined. This has led to the after-party culture these days. After team work, Koreans generally spend time for relaxing so called 'after-party' like drinking and singing together.

There is an old Korean saying 'hell hath no fury like a woman scorned'. This shows how harsh social and cultural conditions Korean women faced. Regardless of nationality and gender, anyone confronting adversity have *han* feelings. *Han* is not an indigenous trait of Koreans just as it is not limited to women. The thing is who hold *han* feeling and what to from it.

Bibliography

Amsden, Alice H. 1989. *Asia's Next Giant: South Korean and Late Industrialization*. Oxford: Oxford University Press.

Buswell, Robert E. 2006. *Christianity in Korea*, Honolulu: University of Hawaii Press.

Cho, Soon. 1994. *The Dynamics of Korean Economic Development, Washington*, D.C.: Institute for International Economics.

Choi, Jang Jip.2005. *Democracy after Democratization*. Seoul: Humanitas.

Choi, Joon Sik, et al. 2011. *Understanding Korean Contemporary Culture*. Seoul: Jimoondang.

Chung, Duck-Koo and Barry Eichengreen. 2004. *The Korean Economy beyond the Crisis*, Aldershot: Edward Elgar Publishing Ltd.

Cumings, Bruce. 2005. *Korea's Place in the Sun: A Modern History*, New York: W.W. Norton.

Deuchler, Martina. 1992. *The Confucian Transformation of Korea: A Study of Society and Ideology*. Cambridge, MA: Council on East Asian Studies, Harvard Univeristy.

Duncan, John B. 2000. *The Origins of the Choson Dynsaty*. Seattle: Univeristy of Washington Press.

Ebrey, Patricia Buckley, Anne Walthall, and James B. Palais. 2009 (2nd ed.). *Modern East Asia: From 1600: A Cultural, Social, and Political History*. New York: Houghton-Mifflin

Eckert, Carter, Ki-baik Lee, Young Ick Lew, Michael Robinson, and Edward W. Wagner. 1990. *Korea Old and New: A History*. Cambridge, MA: Korea Institute, Harvard Univeristy Press.

Em, Henry. "Minjok as a Modern and Democratic Construct: Sin Ch'aeho's Historiography." In *Colonial Modernity in Korea*, edited by Gi-Wook Shin and Michael Robinson, pp. 336-362. Cambridge, MA: East Asia Council Publications, 1996.

Kendall, Laurel.1985. *Getting Married in Korea: Of Gender, Morality, and Modernity*. Berkeley: University of Hawaii Press.

_____, ed. 2002. *Under Construction: The Gendering of Modernity, Class, and Consumption in the Republic of Korea*. Honolulu: University of Hawaii Press. Kim,

Kim, Choong Soon. 2007. *Kimchi and IT: Tradition and Transformation in Korea*. Ilchogak Publishing co., Ltd.

Kim, Kyung Hyun. 2004. *The Remasculinization of Korean Cinema*. Durhan: Duke University Press.

Kim, Young Hoon. 2013. *Understanding World Heritage in Korea: From Dolmen Tombs to Heaven's Gate*. Seoul: Jimoondang.

Lee, Hyangjin. 2000. *Centemporary Korean Cinema : Identity, Culture, Politics*. Manchester: Manchester University Press.

Lee, Jong Won. 2004. *Success and Failure of The Korean Economy and Its Prospects*, Seoul: Haenam.

Pai, Hyung Il and Timothy R. Tangherlini. 1998. *Nationalism and the Construction of Korean Identity*. Berkeley: The Regents of the University of California.

Sakong, Il. 1993. *Korea in the World Economy*, Washington, D.C.: Institute for International Economics.

Seth, Michael J. 2006. *A Concise History of Korea: From the Neolithic Period through the Nineteenth Century*. MD: Row- man & Littlefield.

Shin, Gi-Wook, and Michael Robinson. Eds. *Colonial Modernity in Korea*. Cambridge, MA: East Asia Council Publications, 1999.

Shin, Ki-Young. "Legality Making Gender and Nation in Post-Colonial Korea." *Journal of Korean Studies* 11 (Fall 2006)

Song, Byung Nak. 2003. *The Rise of the Korean Economy*. 2003(3rd ed.). Oxford: Oxford University Press.

The Center for Information on Korean Culture. 2006. *Exploring Korean History through World Heritage*. Seoul: Hollym Corp., Publishers.

Valerie Gelezeau. 2007. *The Republic of Apartments*. Seoul: Humanitas.

Wells, Kenneth. 1990. *New God, New Nation: Protestants and Self-Reconstruction Nationalism in Korea 1896-1938*. Honolulu: University of Hawaii Press.